A BRIEF STUDY

OF GLOBALIZATION

A BRIEF STUDY

OF GLOBALIZATION

Is Globalization Good for People?

Nicholas Dima

This book was printed in the United States of America.

Rev. date: 02/23/2013

To order additional copies of this book, contact:
Xlibris Corporation
1-888-795-4274
www.Xlibris.com
Orders@Xlibris.com
128128

Contents

Preface

When I was giving a lecture recently, a student asked me what I thought about globalization: Is it good or bad for the people? My answer was ambiguous, but the question made me research the subject more deeply. Then, I was asked to teach a full course on globalization, and while preparing the lectures and sharing the notes with a few friends, I was advised to develop them into a printed manual. That triggered a dilemma: In today's world everything has been written and could be found rather easily on the internet. Why compound an already complicated world? Perhaps, it would be for those who do not have the time to sift through the maze of modern information and would appreciate to learn from a concise study. This is how and why I came to write this book.

The study of globalization involves knowledge of several disciplines as well as personal experience. Consequently, this overview is primarily addressed to graduate students, to researchers, to people in politics, and otherwise, to any informed citizens. Therefore, the purpose is to help the readers understand the era of globalization and to prepare them to better confront the future. This study walks the readers through the 20th Century, an era of geopolitical conflict, and leads them to the current era of geo-economic cooperation. Hopefully, they will acquire a better knowledge of the current trends, and this will help them reach their own conclusions about the causes and consequences of globalization.

The study draws upon a number of recent good books, upon many other related sources, and upon the author's knowledge and experience. As methodology, when the course is offered in the classroom, the author recommends interactivity and ample use of examples, video graphs, and power point presentations. Participating students are advised to research their preferred topics and share their own findings.

Introduction

By 1900 the world was split into nation-states and geopolitical spheres of influence and was caught up in unending conflicts and wars. By 2000 the world entered an era of international integrations that gave special meaning to the word "globalization." As a word, globalization entered the common vocabulary in the 1980's and began to represent the economic side of the political concept of "New World Order." However, what does it exactly mean?

There are many definitions and interpretations of the idea of "globalization." According to Steger, for example, globalization is *"a social condition characterized by tight economic, political, cultural, and environmental interconnections and flows that make most of the current existing borders and boundaries irrelevant."* Also, *"Globalization refers to the expansion and intensification of social relations and consciousness across world-time and world-space."* (1) However, globalization is considered an elusive concept and it refers to a process, a condition, and a new age of the world. As a process, globalization is caused primarily by modern technology, but it is driven by politics and economic forces. Furthermore, it is a "global" phenomenon, but it affects virtually everybody "locally." Globalization also represents a serious "shrinkage" of time and space; it results in a strenuous relationship between big Trans-National Corporations (TNCs) and Nation-States; it feeds a conflict between traditional values and yet little known "New Age" values; and it leads to a confrontation between internationalism and nationalism. Thus, while studying the process of globalization certain questions should be kept in mind:

* What are the goals of national governments in the present era?
* What are the interests of TNCs?
* Is globalization a natural phenomenon and an inevitable social trend?
* Where is modern technology and globalization taking us?
* What other alternatives are there for the world?
* Who is winning and who is losing in the process?
* How is the process affecting humanity morally and spiritually?

Philosophically, some of us wonder what is the purpose of our existence and what should we strive for in life? Some people work to make a living and when they have enough material goods they stop working. Others seem to live in order to work and they never stop working. Many people believe that order on earth comes from a divine plan; therefore, there should be a God. Others think that somebody must be in charge here on earth. The risk is that certain leaders may start to act as a god themselves. History is full of them. The waxen mummy of Lenin, as an example, is still kept in his Kremlin mausoleum as an immortal god!

Power corrupts and absolute power corrupts absolutely. This old adage seems to continue to hold true. Is greed part of our human nature? Can human nature be changed? For some people there is no limit for acquiring wealth and power. And when they have it, they may use it for humanitarian purposes or more likely for evil goals. Stalin and Hitler illustrate the case. However, at some point in life we all have to filter our experience, to open our eyes, to use our intelligence, and to ask some basic questions. In this case, the question is simple: is globalization a force for good? We do not know yet. It all depends on the whims of those who are at the top of the world, and this is the risk. Are they fair? Are they wise? What have we learnt from history? Here are some of the thoughts of several wise men. And why do we rely on them? Because as Isaac Newton said *"If I have seen further, it is by standing on the shoulders of giants."* What have we learnt from world giants?

"An imbalance between rich and poor is the oldest and most fatal ailment of all republics." (Plutarch, ancient Roman Philosopher).

"In a situation where there is no righteous person, try to be the righteous one." (Hillel, 1st Century Jewish scholar).

"Nearly all men can stand adversity, but if you want to test a man's character, give him power." (Abraham Lincoln, American president).

"We are all worms, but I believe I am a glowworm." (Winston Churchill, British Prime Minister).

"The only thing that we learn from history is that we do not learn from history." (Georg Hegel, German philosopher). (2)

What have we learned so far from the process of globalization? Hopefully, there should be an answer by the end of this overview.

1 — History and Evolution

ARGUMENTS FOR AND AGAINST GLOBALIZATION

Historically, in the distant past the Middle East was the engine of the world and the region made huge contributions toward the material and spiritual progress of mankind. At the time, the "world" was very much local and regional. Later, the Middle East became the inspiration for European civilization mostly through Greece, which borrowed many of the Middle Eastern ideas and inventions. Then, the Romans took over and made Rome the center of the known world of those days. The fall of the Roman Empire triggered a period of one thousand years of dark ages. Yet, Europe revived and by the beginning of the 16th Century took the world's center stage again. It was in a way the very beginnings of the process of globalization.

The modern world started some 500 years ago with the European Renaissance that led to a "Euro-centric world-view" with global ramifications. And Europe remained in the center of the world until the 20th Century. After the Second World War, the center of the world, at least economically, moved to the United States of America. Currently, the economic center of world activities is slowly moving toward the Pacific region. The modern era, however, was "invented" by Western Europe and accordingly, many European institutions, beliefs, values and attitudes were adopted by virtually the entire world. It all started with the Renaissance, which marked the triumph of science and rationality over the obscurantism of the Middle Ages. It was also the beginning of individualism and materialism. Gradually, the world changed from God-centered to Man-centered. About three hundred years later, the Industrial Revolution that started in England led to the capitalist era. Then, the last century was very much America's century. It was a century of uncontrolled and brutal capitalism at the beginning, struggling and somehow tamed capitalism later, and drifting and unpredictable capitalism more recently. In the process, mankind lost its traditional balance between materialism and spirituality and was thrown into the current state of transition.

Actually, ever since the making of the first tools during the Stone Age, to the invention of the wheel some 5,000 years ago, and on to the present World Wide Web (WWW), mankind has invented and reinvented itself and has been in a continuous state of transition. The difference is that the current transition is rapid and global and many people have difficulties adjusting to it. And while some people are left by the wayside, those who adapt and adjust seem to become increasingly robot-like beings. Our very humanity is at risk. That raises some philosophical questions: Is there an end to our perpetual evolution and transitions? Are we advancing toward higher spiritual selves, or toward self-destruction? Do the architects of the New World Order have a master plan for the future of mankind? What are their ideologies and plans?

Any new ideology or philosophy has to explain the meaning and purpose of life, but does life have a meaning? The architects of the current globalization do not tell us much. And yet, for the advocates of the new trend, globalization is already a new ideology. Ideologies, however, can motivate and mobilize people for great achievements, but also for destructive actions. And as a rule, ideologies always invoke good intentions, but the French philosopher Blaise Pascal warned us that ... *the road to hell is paved with good intentions.*

Globalization is the outcome of several important processes and factors like modern technology, trans-national corporations (TNCs), national governments, international organizations, and people's attitudes and demands. Globalization also reflects an objective reality as well as a subjective one. Modern technology, for example, is an objective reality. It means: computers, mobile phones, satellite communication, internet, TVs, and many other inventions and innovations. They all make us feel as part and parcel of a global world. Objectively, technology expands and stretches our relations, makes us interdependent, and intensifies human relations across time and space. Subjectively, technology shapes our behavior, reshapes our identities, and influences our consciousness. (3) *Volens nolens* globalization marks the beginning of a new human consciousness, but we have a long way to go. Reaching across the globe is rather easy now, but shaping a global identity is still beyond the horizon!

Globalization is strongly influenced and shaped by modern technology. And from all modern inventions, nothing has been more important in the process of unifying us than the semiconductors. They have been around since the 1950's and have developed exponentially ever since. They are the engines of the digital age and have pervasive applications. Though almost invisible, they are now omnipresent and have become indispensable.

In the United States the industry started in the Silicon Valley of California, which is in fact Santa Clara Valley. Currently, the American Semiconductor Industry is dominated by INTEL and AMD. As much as 70 percent of Intel production is done in the US, but Intel is also global and has major facilities in Israel and Ireland. In 1971 Intel made a microprocessor with a capacity of 3,500 transistors. In 2000, it made processors with 400 million transistors. Designing and manufacturing transistors is difficult and expensive. It requires the brain of high-level scientists, intensive research, and huge capital investments. A modern state-of-the-art plant can cost between two and three billion dollars. Only huge TNCs have the resources to build them. (4) From this point of view, modern technology widens the gap between the advanced and the underdeveloped countries, and also between skilled people and assembly-line workers.

Other than that, modern technology has spread like a wild fire. When Apple Computers offered the public the new I Phone 5 in September 2012, many American youngsters waited for a week outside the store doors to buy the new product. And since the youth represent the future and the future belongs to modern technology, we should expect even more globalization. From this point of view, globalization is indeed an irreversible process.

The world is increasingly "global" from an economic point of view, but the development is very uneven and is dominated by a few countries located in three centers. The three centers are Anglo-Saxon North America, Western Europe, and South-East Asia. Some other countries, such as Brazil, India, Mexico, are also moving toward modernization and are pursuing their own global niches, but a good part of the remaining world is pretty much left behind.

Attitudes toward globalization and toward its consequences vary greatly. The advocates of the process insist that in the future everybody will be a winner. The opponents are very skeptical. The opponents claim that the current stage of globalization seems to represent just "a *huge experiment in unleashing economic deregulation and a culture of consumerism on the entire world.*" (5) Such critics fear that the process will lead to serious crises and possibly to self-destruction. Nevertheless, the well-developed countries and their TNCs support the process of globalization since as a rule it works in their favor. The United States has also embraced globalism without any reservation and made "free markets" and "free trade" key priorities of Washington's national security. Other Western countries have been more nuanced and also more ethno-centric. International organizations generally support the process. Many national leaders are caught between a rock and a hard place. Some of them insist on "fair" rather than "free" trade, but defining what is fair and what is free is a matter of interpretation and interest. Developing and poor countries have little or nothing to say and average citizens bear the consequences.

Some time ago, Professor Francis Fukuyama coined the expression "the end of history." Recently, Professor Peter Dicken asked rhetorically: is globalization "the end of geography?" We do not know the answer, but we are in the middle of a global transition. And the globalization process has caused both enthusiastic support, as well as wide-spread opposition. Yet, independent and objective critics warn that unaddressed issues and unchecked social polarization could lead to catastrophic events more dangerous than those of the 20th Century. Thus, is globalization good or bad? So far we only know some of the consequences.

At a general level these consequences are: increasing world domination by rich and powerful countries; economic domination by TNCs; increasing gaps between rich and poor countries; and erosion of national sovereignty.

At a local level, globalization causes a polarization of incomes between very rich and very poor people everywhere; it affects people, places, and countries very differently; it generally creates low-paying jobs; and it causes friction and social problems.

Indeed, the process of globalization has polarized the world. A number of TNCs and a handful of people have become incredibly rich. The rest of the world is not necessarily poorer than before in absolute terms, but it is being left more and more behind. It is therefore a matter of measurable facts, and a matter of perceptions. And perceptions may trump realities.

It should be admitted, however, that globalization also entails some benefits for most people. They are: intensified trade with more goods readily available everywhere; a more diverse production base and reduced production cost; spreading of new technologies; increasing international relations and human contacts; and, allegedly, spreading of democracy globally.

As one can see, there is a trade-off. Economically, people enjoy more goods than before. Politically, however, people must submit to a new world order and to new systems, and often they feel confused. In Europe, for example, the new order comes increasingly from Brussels and often times collide with the old national order. As a result, the process of globalization has caused the world to drift morally toward unknown shores. Furthermore, losing traditional values and beliefs without acquiring new global ones has made many people feel spiritually disoriented. Is this good or it is bad?

2 — The 20th Century
MACHINE-FACTORIES, WARS, AND GEOPOLITICS

The 20th Century was an era of new discoveries, inventions, innovations and diffusion processes. The world was eventually linked together as into a web. The transformation was gradual, but continuous. It involved among others: steam engines, telegraphs, telephones, internal combustion engines, electrical machines, flying machines, computers, space satellites . . . Politically, it was a "short" century of milestone events such as the two world wars, the Bolshevik Revolution of 1917, and the unexpected collapse of communism in 1989. If one judges eras not chronologically, but as values, attitudes and behavior, the wake-up call of the century was the Bolshevik Revolution, and the end of it was the first atomic explosion of 1945 which brought about the nuclear age. It was also a "century" of ideologies: Capitalism, Socialism, Communism, Nazism, and now Globalism. And what are ideologies?

> *"Ideologies are powerful systems of widely shared ideas and patterned beliefs that are accepted as truth by significant groups in society. They offer people a more or less coherent picture of the world not only as is, but also as it ought to be. In doing so, ideologies help organize the tremendous complexity of human experience*

*into fairly simple claims that serve as guide and
compass for social and political action."* (6)

Usually, ideologies are advocated by discontented elites
who manage to manipulate the masses for their own goals.
As a consequence, most of the time ideologies help some
political groups acquire and legitimize power. In this regard,
people must be aware of demagogues with attractive speeches
and populists who promise the "world." Sometimes, people are
tired of them, but indifference or neglect of politics can be as
dangerous as abuse of power. Thus, people must be educated,
informed, mobilized and active in politics. In fact, each political
system and ideology has supporters and apologists, as well as
opponents, and they all vie for political power. And while some
ideologies are radical and dangerous, others are more benign.

Capitalism, for example, is more of a natural way of life
than an ideology and is associated with Western democracies,
and in turn is loosely linked to Christian beliefs. Capitalism
is also a materialistic system, but materialism with a human
touch. As long as the accumulation of capital was held in check
by traditional Christian values, excessive materialism was
frowned upon. However, the rise of Protestantism in Europe
and later the American experience, have gradually led to the
present excessive polarization of wealth. Given the very selfish
nature of man, one may ask: is there any alternative? Churchill
once said that *"Western democracies are the worst forms of
government, except for all the others"* . . .

Capitalism, however, is prone to crises and develops in
cycles. Accordingly, there have been three major stages in

21

the evolution of capitalism: *competitive capitalism, organized capitalism, and disorganized or deregulated capitalism.* Competitive capitalism prevailed before 1900 and encountered little governmental intervention. Organized capitalism dominated the West from the early 1900 till about the 1970s. And deregulated capitalism started in the 1980s and prevails today throughout much of the world.

The United States took the center stage of capitalism by the end of the 19th Century and has remained at its head ever since. A special edition of *U.S. News and World Report* published on April 26, 1982, explained briefly the main events that shaped the American economy. Prior to 1900 there were no rules to restrain economic development and virtually no labor unions to defend the workers. It was during that period that John D. Rockefeller, for example, organized Standard Oil Trust, which at the time controlled 90 percent of all refined oil in America. It was during the same period of time that big monopolies began to exercise excessive control over the economy and over the lives of the American people. The main features of that stage of capitalism were *manufacture and machine-facture, smoke stack industries,* and later *assembly lines and scientific management.*

The concentration of capital and production, however, made the American government worry and prompted Washington to act. As a result, in 1890 the Congress passed the Sherman Antitrust Act with the goal of slowing the growth of big monopolies. Then, in 1913 the Congress passed the Federal Income Tax Law. Taxation was progressive with rates varying initially from 1 percent to 7 percent, and it allowed the government to tax big businesses. Since then, tax laws have changed several times and rates have obviously increased. However, over the years the income tax code has become so cumbersome and with so many loopholes and exceptions, many of them favorable to the rich, that people began to question the equitability of the system. It is a known fact that many middle income Americans pay more taxes than some millionaires. No wonder there are hot debates currently in Washington about taxes.

Competitive capitalism was gradually replaced by organized capitalism, which was efficient from a production point of view, but it led to overproduction and to frequent crises. The biggest of all those crises was the Great Depression of the 1930s. Such crises led to strong nationalistic reactions, especially in Europe, and to calls for social justice and socialism in many other countries. The socialist trends led to Marxism and communism in Russia and to national-socialism and fascism in Germany and Italy. Thereafter, the world lost its innocence. From a social point of view, communism nationalized the entire economic sector while fascism only exercised control over the economy. In other capitalist countries, the state had to intervene and take over some private activities. Yet such actions caused stagnation which compelled the governments to eventually adopt deregulation measures. Slowly, most of the Western capitalist world was deregulated.

Current deregulated or disorganized capitalism is dominated by big trans-national corporations. What happened around 1900 in America is happening now at a global level. But, if Washington could intervene then and prevent the formation of monopolies in the United States, no government has jurisdiction over the world now and practically, nobody can control the big corporations. We do have now a number of global organizations and there are many international negotiations, but they rarely achieve any important accords.

In the meantime, the new global corporations have expanded their reaches in the production process as well as in marketing. They try to occupy every nook and cranny aiming at specific markets and consumers according to the income of the potential buyers. For example, one can buy a pair of shoes for 10 dollars or for 400 dollars; one can buy a pen for 10 cents or for 5,000 dollars; or one can pay 5 dollars or half a million dollars for a watch. In addition, the TNCs can produce in China and market in Canada or can produce in Sweden and market in Indonesia. The only problem is that prices are increasingly similar all over the world for well known brand names, but incomes are astronomically apart. It all started at the end of the last century and it definitely prevails all over now. Furthermore, the huge gap between high-end and low-end prices does not necessarily reflect a corresponding difference in quality. It reflects the abysmal vanity of some people! And we do not know where this new era is going to take us in the future.

From an ideological point of view, communism was associated with Russia, and from the beginning, Marxism had global aspirations. The dream of those internationalist leaders in charge in Moscow was to spread the new socio-political system globally. And the Soviet Union became *a country without a nation that had an army without a country,* whose purpose was to bring Marxist "happiness" to the entire world. Except for some grandiose achievements done with huge human sacrifice, the former Soviet Union was a social failure.

The forced industrialization of the country was done at the expense of agriculture, and the collectivization of the land cost untold tragedies and millions of lives. Despite every efforts and coercions exercised by authorities, human nature could not adapt to communism. Realizing that people did not embrace the new system freely, in 1940 Moscow enacted special laws against "absenteeism, idleness, and sabotage." Accordingly between 1940 and 1955, 36 million people, representing one third of all Soviet adult population, were found guilty. Some of the "guilty ones" were fined or punished locally, but 15 million were sent to prison and 250,000 were shot. (7) Yet, the system did not work because economies based on slave labor are not innovative, do not offer incentives, and cannot prosper. Sooner or later, they are doomed to die.

As for national-socialism or Nazism, the system was associated with Germany and had regional goals. Hitler promised the German people a 500 years *Reich* that would extend from the Atlantic to the Urals. In the end, Nazism filled Europe with concentration camps and together with communist Russia ruined the continent.

Geopolitically, the 20th Century world was multi-polar at the beginning and was dominated by a number of nation-states. The dominant powers in Western Europe were Great Britain, Germany and France. Like any other nation-states these countries secured law and order internally, but vied for international domination and eventually engaged in two devastating wars. By the end of the Second World War the world became bi-polar with the United States leading the West and the Soviet Union controlling the communist camp. Later, the decolonization policy created the concept of the First, Second and Third World, but that did not change the basic bi-polarity balance that lasted until the collapse of the communist east. After the dismemberment of the Soviet Union, by 2000, the world was very much uni-polar with America reigning alone at the top, but that state did not last. Militarily, the United States is still at the top, but economically it is increasingly challenged by powerful newcomers.

Economically, the 20th Century was very much the American Century. In this regard, the period from about 1950 to about 1970 is considered the "American golden age" and the key was its manufacturing industry. Actually, Alexander Hamilton, one of America's founding fathers, insisted more than 200 years ago that a free people should protect its industrial sector because this sector keeps the country independent. Pat Buchanan, a noted journalist and researcher, also wrote recently that "manufacturing is the key to national power." Besides national security, a strong industry provides good jobs for the employees, which in turn brings about national pride and individual dignity. Industry also promotes research and innovation and fosters further development. Yet, currently, following the globalization process, the United States is losing part of its industry and with this it loses many good jobs. (8) Are pride and dignity to follow next?

3 – 21st Century

HIGH-TECH AND NEW GEO-ECONOMIC ARRANGEMENTS

The seeds of the 21st Century were sown somehow in 1945 when the Hiroshima explosion triggered the Nuclear Age. Yet, the most important contribution of the last century to the era of globalization was without doubt the computer. The computer was followed by the space age, which culminated with the 1969 landing on the Moon. Then, the end of the cold war around 1989 led to a new global balance of power. While the cold war is now fading from the memory of many people, the nuclear peril is still with us. Gradually, the "Atomic Club" expanded to include now besides the United States, Russia, Great Britain and France, also China, India, Pakistan, Israel, North Korea, and soon possibly Iran. Is this safe for the future of the world? And who is to decide who should join the club and who should be blocked from becoming a nuclear power? Who has the high moral ground to do so?

For the United States the 21st Century began with a big bang; September 2001 launched the age of modern terrorism on American soil. It was a wake-up call. At the time, I was a visiting professor at the US Naval War College in Newport, R.I. where I witnessed first-hand the profound indignation of many American officers. One of them, a full colonel, even stated that this was the "Pearl Harbor" of the new century, though, a century very different than the previous ones. If the 20th Century wars were very much symmetrical and conventional, the new century wars became asymmetrical and unconventional. Consequently, the traditional wars when two armies would confront each other have been replaced by acts of terrorism and by urban guerilla-type of warfare. And the cost of the new warfare is huge and reflects a cynical new reality.

The United States has by far the strongest military in the world and its defense budget is huge. However, the asymmetry eats a lot of it. As an example, Al Qaeda spent an estimated half a million dollars for the terrorist attack of September 11, but the attack cost the United States an estimated 500 billion dollars or even more by some estimates. As another example, Israel has one of the most modern high-tech military in the world. Maintaining its military edge over its enemies is very expensive, but the country still has problems countering the low-cost low-tech Palestinian challenge. What could be the long-term consequences of such asymmetrical conflicts? What if weapons of mass destruction fall into the hands of some rebellious groups? And what if a deeply polarized world compels the masses to revolt against the current entrenched establishments? The answer is simple: Only God knows!

21st Century technologies are changing the face of the world for the military and civil societies as well. It consists of inventions and innovations of dual use, such as satellite communication, fiber optic cables, or digitalization . . . The "Digital Age," for example, means convergence between computer and communication technologies, great increase in computing speed and capacity, increasing interface between various parts of the internet, broadband communication technologies, and others inventions already in use or currently in the making. As capacity, for example, a single pair of optical fibers can carry these days the entire North American long-distance communication traffic. (9) What a difference from the world of 1900! This indeed means globalization.

In addition, there are currently some 100 geo-stationary satellites in orbit, as well as over two billion mobile phones world-wide. The *U.N. Telecom Agency* estimated that in 2011 as much as 86 percent of the world population had access to mobile phones. And now mobile phones are actually complex tools that have become indispensable to many of us. The same agency also estimated that about 30 percent of the world's seven billion people have access to the internet. The majority of the internet users are concentrated in the developed countries, but the new technology has reached the entire world. With the internet and mobile phones relaying information in real time, and with satellites and TV programs providing instant pictures of remote events, the world has become indeed a "global village." And what does it mean practically? With the increasing speed of transmitting information and correspondingly decreasing cost, many people want to go "global." Little wonder that big corporations aspire to operate globally and to serve the "world citizens."

Could we, however, consider ourselves world or global citizens? Did mankind acquire a global consciousness? According to U.N. studies, only about one percent of the world population is part of this trend, and actually few people have the means to join the select club or "world citizens." Then, who benefits? The answer is many of us, but some of us are benefiting more than others. To paraphrase George Orwell, *we are all equal, but some of us are more equal than others.* What about the rest? Should anyone care for them? And they are the vast majority!

The new century of the new millennium is dominated economically by some 70,000 Trans-National Corporations which have about 700,000 world-wide affiliates. They are currently the movers of the world economy and they challenge the authorities and sovereignty of nation-states. Most TNCs are concentrated in North America, Western Europe, and East Asia. This three-legged economic colossus accounts for 86 percent of world gross domestic product (GDP). America alone still accounts for 25 percent of world industrial production, 30 percent of world services, and 15 percent of world agriculture, but these shares are declining. (10)

Otherwise, Europe is the world's major trading region, China is now the leading industrial manufacturer, and Japan remains an industrial powerhouse. However, other countries are also coming from behind. India, for example, dominates business off-shoring and out-sourcing as call centers, software and data processing. And Brazil has become a major agricultural producer. As for TNCs, they are continuously looking for the best global locations, as well as resources, manpower and markets, and struggle to keep a balance between economic interests and political realities.

4 — The Economic Aspect of Globalization

Economy means the production, exchange, and consumption of goods and services, which most of the time occurs in a given area and within a monetary exchange system. However, there is no economic development without political backing. And politics mean the rules by which a society is governed. Thus, there is a strong synergy between political and economic institutions. Together, they can make a nation flourish and separately they can strangle it. Thus, politics, formulated chiefly by governments, and economics, driven by private forces in capitalist societies, must evolve together to achieve stability and prosperity. (11) Could this be done at a global level?

Modern socio-economic development is being shaped by national governments, by private corporations, and by international organizations. Traditionally, the national governments control the domestic development, but in the new era the border between national and international is rather blurred. If in the past most economies were local and politics were national, their current tendency is diverging; politics still act locally while businesses tend to act globally. Therefore, for a balanced development, the world needs a new international approach. That trend was understood by world leaders and economists at the end of the Second World War and they tried to address it the best they could. It was for this reason that at the end of the war Washington convoked its allies for the United Nations (UN) meeting and for the Bretton Woods (BW) conference.

The UN was initiated at a meeting in San Francisco in 1945 by the allied nations led by the United States and the United Kingdom. However, the new organization reflected very much the structure of the 1945 world and from the beginning encountered problems and difficulties. Yet, the organization worked as long as the hierarchy of the time was respected. With time passing and with continuous enlargements, the international organization became a sort of a debating society.

The chief current problem of the UN is that it does not correspond anymore to the political and economic realities of our times. Both the Security Council and the General Assembly must be changed in order to reflect the 21st Century realities, but there is no agreement on how to change them. Kiribati, for example, a minuscule archipelago with a few thousand inhabitants in the Pacific Ocean, has the same voting rights as India, a country with over one billion people. Also, Japan and Germany, currently economic superpowers, have the same rights as Djibouti. And the efforts to change the UN or to extend the Security Council have so far failed. The truth remains that the UN has as much power as the super-powers allow it to have. In politics, the name of the game is power. In economics, the name of the game is money.

The UN is still in the hands of the five members of the Security Council with veto powers; that is the United States, The United Kingdom, France, Russia and China. The United States remains the most powerful member of the UN, but is slowly losing influence and power. And while economically the world is becoming increasingly global, politically it has remained parochial. There is no synergy between politics and economics at a global level and the world is drifting apart. Politically, mankind is not ready for a "one world government," but economically is moving fast toward globalization.

Economically, the most important event for the evolution of the world after the war was the Bretton Woods Conference, which was held in New England in July 1944. The event was organized by the United States and the United Kingdom to cope with the post-war economic issues and to keep world trade within acceptable limits. The conference gathered 730 delegates from 44 allied nations, but the agenda was set up by Washington, which gave America the upper hand.

From an economic point of view, the Bretton Woods conference established a set of binding rules for post-war activities and created a stable monetary exchange system pegged to a fixed gold value of the American dollar. At the same time, the conference established the International Monetary Fund (IMF) to administer the monetary system, and the International Bank for Reconstruction and Development (the World Bank/ WB) to provide loans for the reconstruction of Europe. Later, the World Bank expanded to provide funds for various projects in developing countries. However, many foreign leaders consider the IMF and the WB to be insensitive institutions which represent mostly the American interests. Indeed, these institutions are located in Washington, DC, close to the White House. Yet, continuing the trend of Western-centered economic activities and in order to better enforce and supervise international trade, in 1947 the General Agreement on Tariffs and Trade (GATT) was formed. In 1995 GATT was transformed into the World Trade Organization (WTO) reflecting the beginning of the current globalization era. Ever since the WTO has imposed strict demands on the signatory countries and has become a very controversial international organization. (12)

These powerful institutions have provided for a long period of "controlled capitalism," but with the process of globalization marching on, international negotiations became acrimonious. These institutions demand that member countries open all their economic sectors to foreign investments, foreign firms be treated on a par with domestic ones, capital and profits movement be unrestricted, and international companies be free to sue the local governments. (13) Such demands and conditions challenge directly the sovereignty of national governments. For example, powerful TNCs request freedom of capital movement without state interference, but the labor movement is controlled by governments. If and when freedom of labor movement will be granted, the role of the nation-state will be drastically eroded and their very *raison d'etre* will be put to test. Who is going to set the rules of interplay between national governments, TNCs and international organizations? Should international organizations pursue the aims of the big and powerful countries, the interests of the TNCs, or the goals of smaller countries and their population?

It is worth mentioning that the architect of the Bretton Woods arrangements was the British economist John Maynard Keynes. He was strongly in favor of state intervention to shape economic development as needed for the people. In this regard, the Bretton Woods system allowed individual countries to control their internal markets and national borders. As a result, through taxation, governments were able to provide social services for their citizens. And for a while, the system worked. However, the Bretton Woods system collapsed after 1971 when President Richard Nixon abandoned the gold-based exchange of the US dollar.

The reality is that the system had become unsustainable in a world that no longer resembled the 1945 reality. Some national systems, such as the one in Great Britain, became overburdened with social programs and the government could no longer honor them. Welfare dependency also became a problem in the United States where some families chose welfare over work. It was a vicious circle. Some people went on public assistance because they could not find jobs, and other chose the welfare system to skirt work. The struggle between business and labor union also had dire consequences on some industries and both sides bear responsibility for the results. Two examples known personally by this author illustrate the point.

Discussion Point: In 1975 I went to work as a reporter for Voice of America. Shortly after being hired we began to focus on the plight of the American steel workers of Pennsylvania who were striking for higher salaries. It took me a while to find out that at the time the steel workers were paid 25 dollars per hour. I had a PhD and my first salary as a government employee was about 8 dollars per hour. The bitter dispute between labor and business could not be reconciled. Soon after, many American steel plants closed down for good. In this case, apparently, the unions killed them. Subsequently, American unions started to lose membership and popular support. About ten years later, however, in 1985, I was appointed as a professor at a military school at Fort Bragg in North Carolina. A local textile factory employing some 300 persons, mostly women, was about to close down. This time there was no union to defend the workers or to push the factory into bankruptcy. It was the beginning of globalization. The factory was supplying textile cloths to only one buyer—the Walmart superstores. But Walmart had found the same products in China for a few cents less per piece than it was paying in North Carolina. For a few pennies, Walmart, an American icon and the biggest retailer in the world, turned its back to the interest of the people! The local textile factory closed for good.

GLOBALIZATION AND LABOR UNIONS

Labor union membership in many Western countries began to decline because on the one hand unions demanded too much, and on the other, companies wanted a free rein on their actions. Unions were strong and needed during World War II and to a lesser degree during the Cold War. In both cases, governments and businesses courted the labor unions to keep the workers on their side. The collapse of communism and the spread of globalization brought down the power and importance of the unions. It was as if after the fall of communism the business community no longer needed the workers on its side.

According to a recent article available on *Google* research and entitled "Trade Union Membership," union membership declined to 29 percent in the United Kingdom, 13 percent in the United States and only 9 percent in France. But, and there is a big but: While France, for example, is approaching a financial cliff, the Scandinavian countries are stable and still prospering. Isn't it interesting then, that union membership in Sweden is 82 percent, in Finland and Denmark is 76 percent, and in Norway is 57 percent? All these northern countries are governed by responsible social-democratic systems able to control and tame their own TNCs for the benefit of their people. They have the highest standards of living in the world and at the same time they provide universal health care, have high quality education, and offer inexpensive university education.

Here in the United States the Health Care reform took many years of harsh debate, public education is in shambles, and access to universities is increasingly for the rich. Who is to be blamed? Trade unions may bear part of the blame for their own downfall, but who is going to defend the employees in the absence of organized labor? Of course, state regulations could do part of the job, but what happens when the state itself is subordinated to big business? This is becoming the new reality in the United States where unions are losing ground and Wall Street has a lot more power than Main Street.

An interesting case of the relationship between labor unions and the government is offered by post-war United Kingdom. During WWII the English people endured quietly many privations waiting for the war to end to address their grievances. Then, the Labor Party came to power with union help and began to create a welfare state. According to the April 26, 1982 special issue of the *U.S. News and World Report*, during the first decades following the war, the government nationalized the steel, transportation, shipbuilding and aerospace industries, and had important shares in the oil and automobile industries. For a while the British economy worked, but it could not sustain for long an extended welfare system. By the time Prime Minister

Margaret Thatcher came to power, England was in a state of economic decline. It was a coincidence that at about the same time Ronald Reagan became president of the United States, during a period when America was also suffering high inflation and high unemployment.

THEORY AND PRACTICE

From an economic point of view, the American economic policy was dominated during the first three decades after WWII by John Keynes' theories. However, by the late 1970's his theories would not work anymore. Subsequently, when President Reagan took over, he joined forces with British Prime Minister Thatcher and resorted to massive privatization and deregulation policies. Slowly, their moves led to a "neoliberal" stand against Keynesian economics and opened the way to the current globalization era. Soon after, huge trans-national corporations began to take over and to transform the world. What followed immediately were economic instability, more stagnation, inflation reaching 18 percent in the US, increased unemployment, public deficits, and many related social ills. Welcome to the era of globalization!

Should governments intervene? Or could the markets regulate themselves as the globalists claim? Economic theories vary and history does not teach us much in this regard. Historically, two British social philosophers, Adam Smith during the 18th Century and David Ricardo during the 19th Century, thought that a liberalized market would tend to balance supply and demand and thus regulate itself. At the time,

Adam Smith claimed in his book *The Wealth of Nations* that any interference by government is almost certain to be harmful. Later, another British economist, Herbert Spencer (1820-1903) added a twist of social Darwinism to such theories. He claimed that free markets are *"forms of human competition in which the fittest would naturally rise to the top."* (14) Nice and Dandy! But what should society do with the old, the sick, the handicap, and the unfit? Should the world let them starve or even "help" them die? And who should decide who shall live and who shall die? Remember, this is what Nazi Germany and Communist Russia did not so long ago.

In today's world having a job is like having the right to live, but only the communist regimes guaranteed everybody a job. And the results were dismal. In the United States the power to "hire and fire" is akin to the power of life or death. One of the biggest political debates these days in America is how to create jobs and reduce unemployment. With regard to "how" to create new jobs, attitudes and opinions are worlds apart. Liberals propose more social programs. Conservatives advocate tax reduction and governmental non-interference. The conservatives have even invented a new word for the rich, calling them "job creators." This is an infantile expression because no private business creates a job for humanitarian reasons; for unrestrained capitalism everything is done for profit! Otherwise, only "demands" create jobs, and the demands for jobs have been moved to China. While in the United States many good industrial jobs were lost, other jobs opened at minimum wage making some folks prefer to go on welfare instead of workfare. And society is indeed caught between a social-welfare kind of system and a return to a sort of human jungle. This trend may lead to a kind of "master and servant" medieval society, but for how long will people endure such a system? At least during the Middle Ages the knights were the first to take up their arms and fight the enemies! The super rich of today take their money and run away.

GEO-POLITICS AND ECO-POLITICS: NATIONS VS. TNCS

The role of the national governments is to control the territories within their borders and to care for all its citizens. By contrast, TNCs insist on opening the borders to enhance their business and profits. At the same time, international organizations try to mitigate the interests of the two and to promote world harmony. One significant step toward globalization promoted by all these three entities is the formation of regional blocs as trade systems. Two important examples in this vein are the European Union (EU) and the North American Free Trade Association (NAFTA). Together, TNCs and the Regional Blocs (RB) act as building blocks of the new global economy.

The TNCs and the nation-states, however, are in a delicate relationship. That means that sometimes they cooperate and other times they compete or even collide. Nevertheless, TNCs and regional blocs help increase world trade, eliminate trade barriers, and increase global wealth. But increasing global wealth does not mean spreading the wealth more evenly around. Advocates of globalization also claim that TNCs and RBs promote better international relations and empower the consumer. Nonetheless, what we see are increased socio-economic polarization and disparity, lower labor standards, ecological degradation and the increase of indebtedness of many countries.

According to the current *World Development Reports* of the World Bank and other recent statistics, the foreign debts of many countries and in particular of the developing or poor countries, are alarming. Furthermore, this international debt has grown exponentially in recent decades. Who is winning and who is losing then? The incomprehensible situation is that even the rich Western countries are indebted, but they will be able to repay their foreign debt. The poor countries will never be able to repay their debts. What will happen then? Or maybe this is the real purpose of the lenders, to keep countries and people indebted forever.

There are many cases of indebted countries worth studying. One such dramatic case is the evolution of the foreign debt of Romania over the last three decades. In 1980 Romania had a foreign debt of about 10 billion dollars. The repressive communist government of Ceausescu decided to repay the debt in full and enacted a special law not to allow the country to ever become indebted again to foreign bankers. With tremendous sacrifices, Romania paid off all its international debt by the time of the so-called revolution of 1989. What followed since is a parody. According to official Romanian statistics, the country is now chained to foreign banks to the tune of over one hundred billion dollars. Statistics, however, can be used, misused and interpreted according to interests. The article "List of Countries by Foreign Debt," available in the *Wikipedia*, mentions Romania with a total foreign debt of 160 billion dollars.

The situation is more or less similar in most East European countries, and Greece, with a debt of 583 billions, as mentioned in the same article, is still on the brink of a precipice. The consequences are alarming for the indebted countries. During the early 2000s, for example, Argentina had an international debt of 141 billion dollars and the IMF forced the country to adopt a very strict austerity program. While the people were totally disoriented, the austerity program made Argentina almost ungovernable. Buenos Aires changed five presidents in two weeks! How can a society survive in such a climate? Who detains the capital? As a former political prisoner, I hate everything communistic, but now I wonder what is the globalist capitalism doing to the world? I realize that I may be stuck in the traditional world of nation-states, but I also understand that the critics of globalization have some valid points.

Critics of globalization underline that nations are created historically in a natural way from the ground up; are located geographically on a given territory; have most of the time common languages and cultures; have governments that at least in principle are elected democratically; and have an inner balance of power between the executive, legislative and judiciary. By contrast, many researchers point out that TNCs are created from above without any popular consent; are "a-territorial" and "a-moral," and feel no national loyalty or local responsibility. They only exist for economic reasons. And if they have any responsibilities, it is to their own CEOs, to their share holders, and to a lesser degree to their employees. Employees, however, are hired and fired as needed.

At the same time, the reality is that no modern corporation can survive for long without showing results. Yet, for the time being, only some people enjoy the fruits of globalization. Corporations are aware of that and promise a better future for everybody. Remember though that the communist regimes promised the millennia of happiness and delivered hell. Critics also fear that if globalization succeeds completely through various acts of expansions, mergers and acquisitions, TNCs will become huge monopolies of various fields dominated by a handful of enormously powerful CEOs. Under such a scenario, average people may end up indeed being dispensable or changeable elements.

The reality is that governments, representing the people in a modern democratic society, are the sole authorities entitled to confront the TNCs. And governments can shape economic development by regulating investments, trade and markets, by creating physical and human infrastructure, by imposing or easing tariffs and duties, by encouraging certain industries and granting them subsidies, by entering preferential trade agreements such as free trade areas, custom unions, common markets, and eventually by allowing economic unions. (15) All these should be done by national governments for the benefit of the country and its citizens. And so far, Japan, South Korea, even China and a few others have done it. Other countries, however, have succumbed to their corrupt leaders and have failed miserably. Russia, one of the most endowed countries in the world, is an example.

Granted, in view of the power and wealth of corporations, the role of the government is not easy. Of the 100 largest economies in the world, 51 are corporations and only 49 are countries. Consequently, negotiations between states and strong TNCs are difficult. Ford Motor Company, for example, negotiated a very lucrative contract to build cars in Spain and Madrid agreed to almost every condition because Ford could have chosen any other south European country. On the other hand, China, with the biggest potential market in the world, played foreign investors against each other and negotiated very good conditions for itself. As a matter of fact, General Motors, Ford and other Western auto companies have established themselves solidly in China under lucrative agreements, but those agreements are also beneficial for China. (16) Thus, the role of the national government is crucial, but the officials must be competent and honest.

As a late example, Ford is currently building a new automobile plant in Chongqing in southwest China. It is the third Ford plant in the same area. The *Arizona Daily Star* of 28 August 2012 reported that the groundbreaking ceremony took place on Monday, August 27. The initial investment was 600 million dollars and the plant should produce 250,000 cars by 2014 and 1.2 million by 2015. Who benefits? In this case both sides! And why do Western companies invest in China? Because hourly wages for auto workers in China are 10 to 15 times lower than in the United States! In this regard, some cynical American executives even suggest that they could bring back the industry only if American wages fall in line with international wages. How would an American worker survive on a handful of dollars a day? This makes again the case for the intervention of national governments.

5 – The Socio-Political Aspect of Globalization

Modern nation-states came into being in Western Europe after the 30-year-war (1618-1648) between the Catholic South and the Protestant North. No side could win the ruinous war and consequently they signed the Treaty of Muenster, better known as the Peace of Westphalia. The peace established the sovereignty of the state which in turn recognized no superior power.

The 20th Century nation-state system is based on President Woodrow Wilson's "14 points" presented at the Paris Peace Conference following World War I. Inasmuch as possible, the new states respected the principle of ethnic self-determination. Thereafter, the nation-states became the cornerstones of the organization of the world, and the system lasted until very recently. However, the new post-colonial countries of the 1960's inherited the territorial shapes of the former colonies regardless of ethnicity, race, or religion. Hence, such countries are states, but they are rarely nation-states. In addition, many such states were unstable and had to endure endless hardships and conflicts, for example, the Congo and Nigeria in the past and Ruanda and Somalia more recently. Actually, Somalia is currently a state only on paper and the perspectives are discouraging. Yet, in spite of a number of failed states, present international order and world organization continue to be based on the nation-state system.

Recently, however, following the process of globalization, the nation-states began to lose their preeminence. National loyalties are also eroding and national territories are becoming less relevant. Actually, in 1990 President George W. Bush declared that the Westphalia Model was dead and announced the birth of a "New World Order." Yet, no one explained what this expression exactly meant. Some people think that it also means a one-world government. (Interestingly, the Latin expression *Novus Ordo Seclorum* is printed on every American one dollar bills making people wonder about the true meaning of some US symbols.)

With regard to the nation-states, many specialists and observers insist that their demise is premature to say the least. Currently, for example, only two percent of the world's population lives outside of their country of origin. It is true that some state powers have been eroded or devolved, but without state authorities the world would be completely chaotic.

THE PREROGATIVES OF THE STATE

The role of the state, defined as a populated territory administered by a governing body, is to keep order internally, to defend the country externally, to maintain good international relations, and domestically, to protect all its citizens. Through taxation and through other means, such as custom duties, levies, state monopolies etc., the state pays for administration, infrastructure, schooling, public health, defense, social services, law and order, environment, the common good, and so on.

Ideally, the national governments should aim at helping the people evenly, but ideals are hardly possible. Such a goal would mean, among others, taking from the rich and giving to the poor, which economically is counterproductive. Again, the communists tried this approach, but instead of helping the poor be better off, they managed to impoverish everybody. How to achieve a more equitable society has been the preoccupation of many well-meaning governments, but finding a solution has eluded most of them. Then, how can modern societies help the poor? To paraphrase an American televangelist, *"the best way to help the poor is not to be one of them."* Or, give everything to the poor and you'll become one of them.

Practically, the best solution to help the underprivileged would be to build a strong middle class and to reduce the gap between the very rich and the very poor segments of the society. This is what the Western democracies have traditionally done. Yet, globalization seems to polarize and to pull our world further apart. It is, thus, the national government that can and should enact and enhance policies that no corporation can. However, governments must keep a well-balanced act in their multiple relations and obligations. They must encourage local businesses; must deal with various TNCs; must respect existing international agreements; and must satisfy the population at large which is called periodically to the polls. A competent government should be able to balance the act, but in the end it is all a compromise. A few examples should illustrate this point.

Discussion Point: In the early 1990s, shortly after the collapse of communism, I interviewed AM, the mayor of the city of Brasov, where the largest tractor factory in Romania was located. That factory and hundreds like it throughout East Europe were bankrupt. A French company wanted to buy the plant to manufacture there competitive tractors at about half the price by comparison with other Western producers. The company, however, needed to lay off about 30 percent of the employees and to modernize the plant. The new government of Romania, made up almost exclusively of former communists claiming to be social-democrats, refused the condition out of fear that they would lose the approaching national elections. The deal was never sealed. Then, I visited Brasov in 2012. The factory was practically a ruin and everybody had lost their jobs. In this case, the opportunism and callousness of the new leaders of the country have destroyed most of Romania's industry.

Another case with a happier ending is the relation between the Finnish Nokia Phone Company and the government of Finland. In 2007 Nokia produced 27 percent of all cellular phones in the world and had 25 billion dollars in annual sales. That was the equivalent of Finland's annual budget. Nokia, however, needed to restructure and reorganize, but it had a strong leverage to influence the government. At the same time, the government wanted to keep Nokia at home to secure employment for the people, to tax it for the benefit of the country, and yet to help the company become even more profitable. Could all these things be done? Finland is one of the least corrupt countries in the world. As a result, in this case, a wise government and a responsible corporation found the best solution for their mutual interests.

Powerful TNCs can influence, control and even "own" national governments. But the governments also have possibilities to influence and control TNCs. This is especially true in the case of big and powerful countries. It is a high-stake game. While nation-states still control their territories politically,

TNCs dominate increasingly international trade and the world's economy. Big international corporations want economic freedom, but they need the governments to secure for them internal stability and a good business climate. In turn, national governments must maintain political stability and economic prosperity in order to avoid potential crises. They need each other, but relations between the two are often uneasy. Yet, with competent and honest leaders, everything seems possible!

America's President Theodore Roosevelt understood the delicate relation between the government and big businesses. It is said that he *"despised the rich, but also feared the poor."* And he busted several big corporations such as Rockefeller's giant Standard Oil. At the time this company controlled 90 percent of US refineries and had a wealth greater than the annual American budget. Aware of the perspectives, President Roosevelt said: *"Great corporations exist only because they are created and safeguarded by our institutions; and it is therefore our right and duty to see that they work in harmony with these institutions."* (17) Can governments control TNCs? To a certain degree only!

According to a Walmart 2010 Financial Report published by *Wikipedia*, Walmart is currently the largest corporation in the world followed by Exxon Mobil. In 2009 Walmart made $401 billion in revenue exceeding the national budget of all but 20 countries in the world. How can small countries negotiate with such giants?

In the United States Wall Street has as much power as the entire American people and it seems that even the mighty US government can no longer control it. Actually, Wall Street makes a very good case. In 2008 Goldman Sachs, a financial institution founded in 1889 and one of the most powerful on Wall Street, had to be saved from collapse by the federal government with taxpayers' money. During the previous year Goldman Sachs had made a profit of 10 billion dollars. That year it paid its employees average annual salaries of 622,000 dollars. The top 25 executives received bonuses of 25 million dollars each, and the chief CEO, Lloyd Blankfein, received 54 million. Yet, they bankrupted the company. When Blankfein was summoned to testify before Congress in a public hearing, he insisted that his corporation should not be held accountable for its decisions. He also rejected any form of governmental oversight and insisted that Goldman Sachs should monitor itself. And who pays for such company errors, speculations or even fraud? The answer is simple, the government with taxpayers' money. It looks like "legitimate fraud," if one could use such an oxymoron, is alive and kicking in today's America.

In the same grain, when the chairman of the Federal Reserve Board, Ben Bernanke, testified before Congress, he did not answer some questions stating that according to the agreement with the government he does not have to divulge the activities of his institution. By the way, the Federal Reserve Board was set up in 1913 when the US Congress delegated to the new bank its constitutional duty to provide a national currency. The Board is indeed federally chartered, but is a private bank which issues the American money. The government does print the dollars for the Feds, but it does not have control over them and, in addition, it pays interest for their use. Then, who controls the money controllers in America and in the world?

While private corporations want to be and very much are on their own, national governments are under the supervision of international organizations such as the IMF, WB and WTO and must follow their directives. In the 1990's these organizations produced the so-called "Washington Consensus" demanding the following from the countries they assist: reduce public expenditure, privatize state enterprises, deregulate their economies, reduce tariffs and liberalize trade; and protect private property. As a result of these conditions, national governments collect fewer taxes with which they finance various social programs. And often times the consequences are dire: unemployment, moral disorientation, social decay, higher lawlessness, increased criminality, drugs and alcoholism, family break ups, homelessness, prostitution, violence, destabilization and the like. (18) By the way, few people know that drug trafficking is one of the biggest businesses in today's "new brave world." And while governments are often helpless in combating social ills, TNC's are washing their hands and continue to pursue ever bigger profits. Is this for the benefit of the people? The answer is a solid No!

6—How America Works and Shapes Global Affairs

The United States was organized from the beginning as a republic (*Res Publica*) . . . by the people, from the people, and for the people. From the very beginning immigrants came to the new land in search of freedom and a better life. To this day, liberty and higher living standards are the hallmarks of America and countless people still try to make it to the new world.

The US Capitol, Center of Legislative Power. Source: Wikipedia

From the outset, the founders of the new country provided for a balance of power between the three branches of the government, Executive, Legislative and Judiciary, and guaranteed freedom of the press. Slowly, however and without any invitation, the financial circles began to tilt the initial balance of power. Now Wall Street is a force to reckon with. Extremely rich Americans and even wealthy non-Americans are exercising more power now than ever over the US government. Probably the robber barons of the late 19th Century had more influence over American politics, but at least those "barons" built the country. By contrast, now rich Americans invest overseas, deposit their wealth in foreign accounts, and increasingly they consider themselves global citizens. Why so much concentration of wealth and what do rich people do with their money? Some of them enjoy unimaginable material life-styles; others keep investing to make even more profits; a few donate to charitable organizations; but many of them buy political power.

In the United States there are currently 40 senators who are millionaires. And why do they want to serve in Washington when private corporations pay 10 to 100 times more than any governmental position? They want to do it for prestige and fame and because once in Washington they acquire the power of the governmental institution. From such positions, they set agendas and allocate American resources. And after retiring, they are often hired by big corporations for huge salaries. Yes, it is good to be a high governmental official in America! Big corporations pelt such officials with various favors. Actually, corporations finance the campaigns of many politicians with millions of dollars. It is a vicious cycle. "Money becomes power and power translates into money." For honest politicians it is increasingly difficult to fight big money. After leaving the White House Harry Truman was offered a very lucrative position with a big company. He refused the offer by saying "*You do not want Harry Truman. You want the former president and he is not for hire.*" Few people have the power to resist temptations these days and presidential campaigns have become financial races.

The Masonic Temple of downtown Washington, DC.

Source: Wikipedia

Traditionally, a presidential campaign costs hundreds of millions of dollars. Actually, the *Associated Press* of 8 September calculated that the 2012 campaign was expected to cost two billion dollars when super PAC (Political Action Committees) donations were added. Big corporations have contributed greatly to the campaigns, especially after the Supreme Court's decision that "Money represents Free Speech." (See court case of Citizens United). And there are many ways to support a candidate. Mark J. Leder, for example, an American multimillionaire, organized a fundraiser at his mansion in Boca Raton, Florida, for candidate Mitt Romney. The cost of a dinner plate was 50,000 dollars per person! According to the *Philadelphia Inquirer* of 24 September 2012, it was there that Romney disparaged the 47 percent Americans who allegedly do not pay federal taxes. Such events are attended by very rich people and by corporation executive officers (CEOs).

And why do big corporations donate and make contributions to presidential candidates? Because, among other perks, once elected, the president has the right to appoint about 3,000 persons to influential positions. (Some 30 years ago the president could appoint only 600 persons, but big business made sure it could staff any new administration with its own men and lobbied to increase the number of political appointees). Most of the appointees are highly educated and knowledgeable and become powerful connections for whoever is behind them. By comparison with such informed persons, average Americans know little about the big world and are mostly interests in their daily needs. By the way, 60 to 70 percent of all Americans have never had a passport and have never gone abroad. (Actually, answering a poll about visiting foreign countries, an American said that he had visited Canada and California!) Since the elected officials reflect the average citizens, many times they also know little about world affairs and need to rely on advisers. As a result, often times the appointed officials become the real brain behind the throne. And overwhelmingly, appointees come from private businesses and are connected to such organizations as the Council for Foreign Relations (CFR), Trilateral Commission, Skull and Bones, Bilderberg group, and the Free Masons. A far cry from the *res-publica* envisioned by the founding fathers!

About Some Secret Organizations

The Free Masonry is allegedly an ancient organization which was revived in England in 1717. Currently, it has about 4 million members world-wide and 2 million members in the United States. Most of them are old and the organization has lost its former appeal. American Masonry is still active, but is now chiefly a fraternal organization known for humanitarian activities.

The Masonic Temple of Northern Virginia. Source: Wikipedia

The Bilderberg Group is another prominent organization that started in 1954 at the hotel with the same name in the Netherlands. The organization gathers European and world elites in secret annual meetings where they make global decisions. They also invite known journalists, but the journalists are sworn to secrecy. In 2006 they met in Kanata, a small place in Ontario, Canada. As cited by Rothkopf in his well-documented book *Superclass*, they discussed among other important things the future merging of the US, Canada and Mexico, and how to better reorganize and control the world. Their critics are afraid, however, that their model of social organization is the middle ages when the world was divided between aristocrats and serfs and there was no freedom and no democracy. Members of this group and of the other secret organizations claim that they only provide connections and opportunities, and otherwise, they have the best intentions. A number of American authors and TV programs have focused recently on these secret organizations and their disproportionate power. (19)

American organizations, such as the Council on Foreign Relations (CFR) and the Trilateral Commission, are the best known. The CFR was created in 1921 by a group of academics who advised President Woodrow Wilson, and it is probably the most important of all. Presently, the CFR provides many high-level advisers to government officials. Its headquarters is located in New York City, but it has branches in other countries as well. The Trilateral Commission was created by David Rockefeller in 1973 as a forum to bring together leaders of the United States, Western Europe and Japan. At the time, Rockefeller was also chairman of CFR, Chief Executive Officer of Chase Manhattan Bank, and a prominent member of the

Advisory Board of the Bilderberg Group. One can see real connections!

CFR Headquarters. New York City.

Another secret organization is the Skull and Bones Society. This group was created at Yale University in 1832 to bring together like-minded male students. The two former presidents Bush were active members of the society. Membership is by invitation only and it involves some strange rituals. Among others, they follow "barbarian time" which is five minutes ahead of regular time. (20) These secret or semi-secret organizations and societies work as a "old boys" network helping and promoting each other. They provide a high number of appointees to various governmental positions and also work for important TNCs.

Once in the government, the new appointees press for legislation favorable to the big business community. Actually, many of them are lawyers and help the legislators write the new laws. And legislation is often written in a language that non-specialists cannot possibly understand. Take the US tax code as an example. It contains four million words, which is almost one thousand times the number of words in this book. Furthermore, only since 2001 Congress made some 5,000 additional changes to it. Only specialized lawyers and accountants can understand the tax code which is full of loop holes and provisions used mostly by those who can afford it. It is an open invitation to cheating and everybody does it, but it is "legal cheating" written into the law. As reported by the press during his 2012 presidential campaign, Mitt Romney's family, for example, deducted from taxes 70,000 dollars which they spent for a dressage horse. Most Americans do not make in one full year the amount of money deducted by some people for one item only. The truth is that most US laws are written by specialists and appointees first and foremost for the benefit of big business. Then, after working for the government, the same appointees who have helped to write the new laws often return to work for the large corporations.

Dick Cheney, for example, was US vice president under President George W. Bush junior after being Secretary of Defense under President George Bush senior. At the time of his appointment as vice president, Cheney was working for Halliburton, an American defense contractor. After only five years with that company, he was given 25 million dollars as a retirement fund. (As a mid-level federal employee my retirement fund was about 250,000 dollars after 26 years of work). Then, when Cheney was vice president during the Iraq War, Halliburton obtained a very lucrative business contract in Iraq overcharging the federal government huge amounts of money for its services. The American press noticed the conflict of interests and the government initiated an inquiry into this murky relationship. The investigation did not get anywhere and the case was eventually dropped.

From a military point of view, the connection between government and big business is also very illustrative. In 2010 America's defense budget was 711 billion dollars, which was more than the rest of world combined. According to *SIPRI Yearbook—2012,* during the same year, China had a defense budget of 143 billion, Russia spent 72 billion, the United Kingdom and France spent about 63 billion each, and India's military budget was 49 billion dollars. Currently, the US military has about ten thousand nuclear warheads and 2.5 million soldiers. In addition, there are also many "private armies" which supplement the official American military. In view of this enormous might, some observers have concluded that the American military is built around the idea of permanent war . . . or probably to protect and promote the process of globalization. Rothkopf even suggests that the extreme measures taken in Washington, such as the so-called Patriot Act, and the excessive airport searches, are actually meant to control the population and to keep it in line. (21)

The Defense Department is not the only one interested in a large military budget. The Pentagon works with big defense contractors, which underlines the link between the government and the big corporations. According to *Wikipedia's* article

"Top 20 Defense Contractors," in 2010 the largest receivers of government contracts were Lockheed Martin, Northrop Grumman, and the Boeing Company. Many of the CEOs of such companies used to work for the government and they have learnt the Washington ropes. Is anything wrong with the system? No, if you are in the loop! However, what about the middle class? What about the multitude of those left out?

AMERICA'S MIDDLE CLASS

To a good degree, the press is free in the United States and most journalists are professional and responsible. At the same time, many government agencies and private institutes analyze continuously various aspects of the American society and publish their results. One such topic of study is the situation and evolution of the middle class. To begin with, America tries to put a price or a number on almost everything. How much is a life worth? How much insurance should one person buy? What does it mean from a monetary point of view to be part of the poor, middle class, or upper class, etc. In some cases, definitions and figures are objective and are provided by the government. In others they are subjective and open to interpretation. Currently, for example, if a family of four makes 22,000 dollars per year, it is considered to be living under the poverty line. Other research institutes use different criteria and come to slightly different conclusions. However, the overall conclusion is the same; the American middle class is losing ground.

According to a recently published study made by the *Pew Research Center* and based on 2010 government statistics, to be part of the American middle class a family of three needed a household income of between 39,000 and 118,000 dollars per year. It is a rather wide span, but the middle class is further divided into three categories: lower, middle-middle, and upper middle class. Nonetheless, the study found that:

* Fifty percent of all American adults fell in the middle class category, but this proportion was decreasing. In 1970, for example, 62 percent of all Americans fell into the middle class category.

* According to the same research, most middle class Americans began to believe that hard work was no longer a guarantee of getting ahead and they were afraid that the future generation would not be able to keep their parents' standard.

* The Pew Research Center also found that average income levels have fallen in recent years for most people. And, the disparity between rich and poor has widened.

* Between 2000 and 2010, for example, the median income of the middle class fell from 73,000 to 69,500 dollars.

* According to data reported by the *Associated Press* on 22 and 25 August 2012, the 2009 recession was the biggest since the Great Depression. And apparently it is not over yet.

* As for the individuals affected directly by the recession, only 15 percent of those who were laid off in 2008 found jobs later at similar pay. Most of those who did find new jobs after losing the old ones were paid 20 percent lower salaries.

*	Interestingly, 62 percent of Americans blame the Congress for this situation and 54 percent blame the banks and the financial institutions. Little wonder the *Occupy Wall Street* movement exploded in 2010. Was it an omen for the times to come?

One of the causes of this new trend is the process of globalization, which brought about the migration overseas of many well-paid American jobs. On 23 August 2012, *Reuters* reported that between 2001 and 2011, following a huge US trade deficit with China, America lost 2.7 million jobs and 77 percent of them were in manufacturing. Meanwhile, in 2011 the US trade deficit with China hit a record high of 295 billion dollars. Part of this deficit was fueled by Beijing's policy of lowering the value of its currency, but most of it has been caused by China's industrial activity. Indeed, China has become the world's second largest economy, having raced past Japan in recent years. And while China and other newly industrialized countries strive on producing physical goods, many American businessmen strive on financial speculations.

The Washington Post reviewed in its edition of October 28, 2012, a recent book by Hedrick Smith, a well-known journalist and writer. The very title of the book, *Who Stole the American Dream*, and the title of the review, *The Long Painful Decline of the Middle Class,* by Professor Frederick Lynch, speak volumes by themselves. Smith underlines that "*America's plutocracy has largely abandoned even the pretence of stewardship, loyalty or patriotism.*" The author points out what is now already common knowledge. In order to pursue bigger profits corporate chieftains have moved abroad many of the well-paid American jobs and *"have transferred overseas much of our knowledge-based economy."* According to the reviewer, the author blames this situation on *"the evolution of a Washington-Wall Street symbiosis that dominates White House and congressional policymaking that thrives on political gridlock."* Actually, the very first issue of 2013 of the *Economist* summarized the American gridlock in one sentence printed on its January 5 cover "A broken system, a lousy deal and no end in sight." No wonder most Americans blame Congress and Wall Street for this sad reality!

Discussion Point: A certain explanation is needed here to better understand the plight of the American middle class. For those who may think that making two or three thousand dollars per month is a good salary, one should know some of the American prices. For example, the monthly rent for a modest apartment in an average neighborhood in New York City is over 2,000 dollars. Add to this utilities, telephone, transportation, car insurance (if you can afford a car) and see if you can make it. The situation is similar in most of the large American cities where jobs are available. There are of course towns where one can rent a place for several hundred dollars a month, but there are no jobs available in such cities.

When I migrated to the United States in 1969, I found a job in a department store for the minimum wage of 2 dollars an hour. With that pay I could afford a decent efficiency in uptown New York City for 74 dollars a month. The basic rule in those days was that a week's salary was about enough to cover a monthly rent. Now, the minimum hourly pay is 7.25 dollars and the monthly rent for the same apartment that I rented in 1969 is about 1,500 dollars. Assuming that one works full time at a minimum wage, he or she can make just enough to pay the rent. What about the rest? At the other end of the spectrum, a new apartment at Trump Plaza downtown New York costs several million dollars with some of them exceeding any imagination. I am part of the solid American middle class and enjoy a comfortable life, but this is no longer the country that I came to. What happened?

7 — Super Rich and Dangerous Polarization

What does it mean to be rich? From a financial point of view, apparently, one is rich when he or she has enough money to stop working. At that point people can enjoy everything they desire and can concentrate less on accumulating more money. Yet, asked about how much money a millionaire needs to have enough, John D. Rockefeller answered . . . *"A little more than what he has!"*

Material wealth has always been important to people, but is not everything in life. Who is rich and who is poor may then become a rhetorical question. It depends on what we want in life and from life. For some people wealth as money is everything. For others, wealth is a more subtle issue. Popular lore all over the world offers us adages that speak volumes. "Money talks" and people "follow the money" in the US. Yet, "money can buy medicine, but cannot buy health." Then, who is rich and who is poor?

According to an Indian proverb, *"rich is the person who always has enough and poor is the one that never has enough."* According to *Forbes* magazine, Warren Buffet is currently the second richest man in the world after Bill Gates. They are both incredibly generous with their wealth and Mr. Buffet donated 31 billion dollars to charities. These two men did what two thousand years ago the sage man Hillel advised chosen people to do: *"In a situation where there is no righteous person, try to be the righteous one."* Gates and Buffet have achieved indeed global consciousness, but unlike the evil consciousness of many international corporations which want to exploit everything at a global scale, such men have arrived at a global humanitarian (and Christian) consciousness. This should be the ultimate purpose of humanity!

Warren Buffet (left) and Bill Gates (right). Source: Wikipedia

Indeed, unlike most wealthy people who flaunt ostentatiously their wealth, billionaire Warren Buffet lives in the same three-bedroom home in Omaha, Nebraska, that he bought when he married 50 years ago. Also, he drives his own car and travels by regular planes although he owns the largest private jet company in the world. Unlike his peers, he does not socialize with the high society crowd and lives an ordinary life. And this extraordinary man has some good advices for the young people of today: Stay away from credit cards; live a simple life; do not go for brand names; do not waste your money on unnecessary things . . . As per one of many articles on *Google* research and *Wikipedia*, Buffet said that *"the happiest people do not necessarily have the 'best' things. They simply appreciate the things they have."* Warren Buffet discovered alone what Christianity has been preaching for two thousand years and what Hinduism has known for over three thousand years.

Businessman and philanthropist Warren Buffet. Source: Wikipedia

Can money make people happy? Not exactly, but it sure helps. In this regard, scientists have concluded that happiness is 80 percent inborn; it is genetic. Happiness depends on many factors and money is not necessarily the most important of them. Interestingly, a recent study reported by the *Associated Press* on

December 20, 2012 found the happiest people in the world in Panama, Paraguay, El Salvador, and other rather poor countries from a monetary point of view. At the same time, some of the "richest" countries in the world, such as Singapore, were among the least happy. How right the great Chinese thinker Confucius was when he said that "*Money sometimes prevents troubles; too much money breeds it.*" (22) And the actor turned politician, Arnold Schwarzenegger once said jokingly: "I have 50 million dollars and I am not happier than when I had 48 millions." Well! It takes a certain amount of money to satisfy your needs. More money than that it can bring you problems. The world is full or sad rich and famous people!

Many "driven" notables who became filthy rich gave their money away later in their lives. Andrew Carnegie was one of them. He even said: "*the man who dies rich dies in disgrace.*" At the end of his life Carnegie became a philanthropist, but he had been a ruthless businessman most of his life even with his own employees. In 1901 he sold his company to J.P. Morgan for 480 million dollars and donated the money to schools, libraries and to other causes. Yet, one of his Pittsburgh steelworkers who at the time could barely make a living, wondered: "*what use has a man who works 12 hours a day for a library?*" For his part, Morgan was so ruthless in organizing his production for maximum profits that in his time the word organization became "morganization."

AN INTERNATIONAL UPPER CLASS

Rothkoph wrote that the process of globalization has created an "*international upper class of people whose economic interests have more in common with each other than with the majority of people who share their identity.*" (23) And to make a sarcastic comment, it seems that this is a reversal of the Marxist adage "*proletarians of the world unite!*" It now sounds like "rich people of world unite!" Is this what modern humanity needs?

Currently, there are three billion people (almost half of the world population) who live on less than 2 dollars a day. By contrast, the super rich live in a different world and socialize mostly among themselves; many of them reside in segregated communities with private guards and electronic surveillance; they attend exclusive private clubs, resorts and restaurants; and they network overwhelmingly within the group. Also, overwhelmingly, members of the global financial elite want exclusive places for their ilk, global reach, and access to other rich and powerful people. (24) As an example, J.P. Morgan was attending a meeting of bankers when a young businessman approached him and asked for a loan. "*I will give you something much better*" Morgan answered. He walked with the young man among the bankers, patted him on the back, talked to him, and said: "*Now you can get a loan from anyone here*" . . . (25) Speaking of power of money and connections!

There are about one thousand billionaires in the world and many of them are big CEOs. They are described as ruthless, driven, monomaniacal, and very greedy. Some of them enjoy more powers than country presidents or prime ministers. This super rich class proves Pareto's principle: "*The rule of 20 percent vs. 80 percent.*" Twenty percent of all causes are responsible for 80 percent of all consequences; 20 percent of the world's population controls 80 percent of all world wealth . . . In fact, only 1 percent of the world population controls 40 percent of all wealth. And to be among the 1 percent one must have millions. America has currently circa ten million millionaires. Yet, this does not make one rich; it only makes one financially comfortable. To be truly rich, one must be a multi-millionaire. However, there are financial elites within financial elites. For example, the top one percent of all American households exceeds the combined wealth of the bottom 95 percent of all US households. Furthermore, between 1980 and 2000, the average salaries of large corporations CEOs became about 400 times higher than those of average workers. (26)

All that while a record number of Americans, 46.7 million to be exact, were on food stamps as of 2012. As reported by the *Bloomberg News* of 4 September 2012, California and Texas, the most populous states and two of the richest in the US, had the most food stamps recipients in 2012. And food stamps cost America 76 billion dollars annually.

New Social Polarization

It is worth mentioning that with regard to financial polarization, the ancient Greek philosopher Plato said that the common good of mankind requires a ratio of 5 to 1 between the richest and the poorest members of society. Then, last century, even J.P. Morgan thought that bosses should make 20 times more than their workers. And what happened? By 1900 people in rich countries were paid up to ten times more than in poor countries. And then, according to the 2000 edition of the *U.N. Human Development Report,* the income ratio between rich and poor countries was 44 to 1 in 1973 and it increased to 74 to 1 in 1999. By early 2000 that ratio was about 100 to one. Is this fair? In addition to the financially super rich, there are also a few thousand very powerful people in the world. They are political leaders, prominent academics, renowned thinkers, as well as a number of famous artists, writers and journalists, who also enjoy money, influence and power. As a rule, members of the famous and the super rich group work behind closed doors, avoid publicity, and try not to wake up people's patriotism and nationalism. Yet, this "can lead to catastrophic divides."(27)

It is useful to open a parenthesis here for a comparison with the now defunct Soviet Union. The former communist country also had its own elite called the nomenclature. However, only the Soviet political nomenclature had money and power. The intellectual, scientific, technical and artistic elite only enjoyed money and a higher standard of living. However, members of the non-political elite were aware of the inequity and instability of the system which eventually collapsed. It appears that today's super rich class lives in a world of its own as the aristocratic class of Russia did before the earth-shaking Bolshevik Revolution.

8—The Demographic Aspect of Globalization

A huge problem in today's world, which apparently worries the political and economic leaders of the Western countries, is the current trend of demographic evolution. Indeed, the population of the globe has increased dramatically in recent times. Historically, it reached 1 billion people by 1825; 2 billion by 1925; 4 billion by 1975; 6 billion by 2000; it is over 7 billion now; and it will reach some 10 billion by 2050. Is this growth sustainable? When I did my graduate studies at Columbia University in the early 1970s this growth was viewed with alarm.

This dramatic population increase was possible mostly because of the Western inventions and discoveries of the 19th and 20th centuries. Great achievements in biology, medicine, hygiene, as well as higher standards of living, led to a big decrease in infant mortality and to a substantial increase in longevity. Take hygiene, for example. During the Middle Ages most Europeans would take one bath per year, usually in the spring. The queen of England bragged about taking a bath every three months. Even now, rural people in some poor countries bathe themselves once a year. Compare that with America where "cleanliness is godliness." As a result, life expectancy in the United States, for example, increased from 30 years in 1800, to 47 years in 1900, and to 78 years in 2000. Actually, according to the *Economist* of December 15, 2012, between 1970 and 2010 life expectancy has increased by 12 years for women and by 11 years for men.

How long could people live and what will be the social consequences, locally and globally, of an increasing and aging population? Does the earth have a maximum carrying capacity? Can societies feed adequately their populations, find employment for all their members and care for an ever increasing population? Or will the world end up in never ending conflicts, epidemics and chaos? Are there already too many people in the world? Who has the right and the power to decide about such a global issue?

Interestingly, an enigmatic stone monument erected by an unknown organization in 1979 in Georgia offers a number of guidelines to the people of the planet. These guidelines or recommendations are carved in stone in eight modern languages of wide circulation. One of them on the frontispiece is also carved in four ancient languages, one of which is Babylonian. The granite monument is rather simple, but at about 19 feet tall (6 meters) is quite impressive. The visitor is left with the impression that something grave might happen to the earth, but apparently humanity will survive. Strangely, the first among those recommendations is to keep the world population under 500 million. The exact wording is *"Maintain humanity under 500,000,000 in perpetual balance with nature."* However, what would happen or could happen to the rest of over 90 percent of the existing people?

The leaders of the world and the sociologists are divided with regard to the demographic future of the planet. Religious people spearheaded by the Catholic Church believe that the matter should be left to God to decide. Yet, the consequences will be borne by all of us and could be very risky. Secular scientists insist that mankind must take the matter into its own hands and put an end to unchecked population growth. The danger is that in trying to impose their views, some leaders would actually acquire god-like powers of life and death over people. China took this approach to the extreme with its one-child policy, but the consequences were only partially successful and not acceptable to most people.

The mysterious Georgia Guide Stone.

DEMOGRAPHY, PEOPLE AND CULTURE

Population studies are dry and full of heartless statistics. Peoples' lives, however, represent individual destinies. We know that the well-studied Demographic Transition concept explains adequately the recent population explosion. However, once humans are born they are no longer statistics; they become real persons. They must be taken care of, must be educated, and must be given some skill to be able to make a living on their own. In the absence of local economic opportunities, young people will either migrate to any attractive places or will create huge social problems at home. It happens all the time.

When people migrate to new countries with different cultures, they usually bring with them their old habits, such as social attitudes, native religious beliefs, and different family and work ethics. From a cultural point of view, religion and faith are still very important traits of the population. When people with traditional beliefs from the Middle East, for example, migrate to the secular Western Europe, the clash of cultures is almost imminent. Max Weber, an early 1900's sociologist, remarked that capitalism is replacing God with devotion to the dollar while modern science is turning people away from God. (28) Currently, while the West is increasingly secular, the Middle East is turning increasingly toward religion. And the two may end up in a clash of civilizations. Religion continues to be important even in the era of globalization, pushing some regions and divided countries toward dangerous collisions.

There are currently some 2 billion Christians, amounting to 32 percent of the world population; 1.5 billion Muslims, representing 23 percent of the world population; and over 1 billion Hindus and Buddhists. There are also many people of other religions who believe in God and who behave accordingly. If we are now living in a globalized world, can we live together in harmony? Recent history offers us little hope. Israel and Pakistan were created based on religion and Ireland was divided between Catholics and Protestants also according to their religion. Yet, Israel is continuously under siege by the Arabs and Pakistan and India are permanently at odds. These three countries are threatened by radical or Muslim fundamentalists. The truth is that radicals are a minority among the Muslims, but these days well-organized minorities menace much of the world. Other than that, demography could very well be destiny. In this regard Israel is faced with a difficult dilemma. It must decide rather quickly about accepting a Palestinian state alongside the Jewish state. Otherwise, it has been calculated than by 2016 the Arabs would outnumber the Jews and thereafter the Arabs would dominate numerically the Israel-Palestinian lands.

Addressing various minority problems is essential for the fairness and stability of the world. Nevertheless, currently it is no longer "politically correct" to speak of various minorities and to stress the problems they sometimes create. Actually, it is frowned upon even to allude to such problems. However, is it correct for radical Muslims, for example, to create a parallel society in France, to refuse to adapt to the new country, and to threaten the traditional French culture and society? London, as another example, is fast becoming a non-English city, but will the future metropolis retain its homogenous culture or it will break apart along cultural, ethnic, or religious lines? Minorities of various kinds add salt and pepper to any society, but what if the needed amounts and proportions get out of balance? Why is it "politically incorrect" to raise questions related to minorities? In fact, it is very incorrect to force people to abide by the so-called "correct "speech. This is more than a straight jacket to freedom of expression. It is plain and simple censorship!

Do majority populations have any rights anymore, or must they succumb to the demands of various minorities? And I am not speaking of racial or ethnic minorities, but of majorities within any group. The honest and hard working majorities! Yes, they should respect their minorities, but minorities must also remember that they have obligations toward the majorities surrounding them. Otherwise, problems will accumulate and the tide of history might turn again against them.

A case in point is provided by the Gypsies in East Europe and in the West when they move there. The Gypsies raise some urgent issues that should be confronted honestly and should be addressed properly. To begin with, Gypsies do not represent a color of the skin, but a separate culture. Begging, cheating and stealing are a way of life for too many of them and spending time in prison is alarmingly common among them. Yet, many Gypsies are resourceful and talented in a number of pursuits. If properly educated and offered adequate jobs, they would become constructive members of any society. Unfortunately, the southeast European countries, where many of them come from, do not have the cultural power or the economic capacity to integrate them. If the European Union is serious, it should stop lamenting about their behavior and it should start to educate and integrate them. In the meantime, increasing numbers of East European Gypsies are attracted by the lure and promises of the West.

Another important demographic aspect of globalization is the tendency of labor to move where there are employment opportunities. In this regard, Western countries want to control the flow and to accept the best and most fit migrants. They have a point. Unchecked population migrations create social problems, but regulated migrations can be mutually beneficial. For example, with fewer people in the labor force, Western countries need immigrants to sustain their economies. And while helping Western economies, foreign workers help their countries of origin by sending home handsome remittances. It is a mutually advantageous arrangement. For example, according to the *Wikipedia* article "Remittance-Top Recipient Countries," in 2010 India received 55 billion dollars, Mexico received 23 billion and the Philippines received 21 billion. These remittances make huge differences and literally help some countries survive. The situation may be mutually beneficial for now, but a better solution would be to create employment opportunities at home, because migration represents a brain-drain and a loss of the best people in many developing countries. Take East Europe, for example. Some 20 million people have left for West Europe during the last two decades and many of them were professional people, thus depriving their countries of some of the best youth.

While for the small East European countries the problem is potential "depopulation," for a big country, such as China, the problem is "overpopulation." From a demographic point of view, China with a population of 1.3 billion people makes a good case study. When the communists took over in 1949, Mao Zedong encouraged the people to have more children. The new Chinese leaders denounced any contraceptive methods and considered them a capitalist plot. As a result, for about two decades a typical Chinese family had up to six children and in time the population doubled. However, periodically, millions of people died because of recurring droughts and starvation.

In 1979 the new Chinese leader Deng Xiaoping realized the danger of uncontrolled population growth and resorted to a "one-child" policy. Incentives and punishments were introduced and the new policy was applied brutally. Over the next decades the population was somehow stabilized and coupled with industrial development it brought about a degree of prosperity to many families. On the negative side, however, the one-child policy coupled with massive migration to cities caused social and family problems. With the "only child" gone to find work in far-away places the elderly parents began to suffer and they had no one to care for them. That prompted the government to enact a strange law. According to *the Associated Press* and as reported by the *Arizona Daily Star* of December 29, 2012 the Chinese national legislation amended a family law requiring adult children to visit their aged parents or risk being sued by them. I wonder if there is any other similar law in the world!

The Chinese population is currently still growing, but in a more manageable way. But, the one-child policy has created a host of unforeseen social and economic problems. Among others, it created an unnatural imbalance between young males and females because traditionally the Chinese prefer sons. More recently, the fear that not enough children will be born in the future to man the industrial development of the country made the Chinese leadership review the one-child policy. In this vein, *Los Angeles Times* reported on 26 August 2012 that Beijing began to reexamine its policy and may allow more than one child per family. If currently, one in five people in the world is Chinese in the future we should expect even more of them.

9 — Cultural and Ecological Problems

The process of globalization also causes cultural and ecological problems and controversies. Culture is an essential trait of humanity, but is a complex concept. Anthropologically, it encompasses the entire human experience, including language, literature, music, science, religion, etc. which are forms of expression. Some of these human expressions have become universal on their own and have been accepted by the entire world as a natural trend. Music of all sorts and classical literature are two such examples. Other forms of culture have been imposed by modern media. All in all, culture is essential for any society to remain viable, to survive and to prosper. As for the environment, ecological problems know no borders. By their very nature they are international and increasingly global. Consequently, ecological issues are already analyzed and treated at different international levels. With regard to cultural issues, nothing has stirred more controversy recently than the global spread of English and the American pop culture.

ENGLISH AND THE AMERICAN POP CULTURE

In recent decades English has become increasingly the *lingua franca* of the world. At the same time, American pop culture has virtually invaded the world, but the trend is being perceived as cultural imperialism rather than cultural globalization. And the two trends, English and the American pop culture reinforce each other. Currently, a great deal of information comes from the United States and is relayed in the English language. This is considered a natural trend and is not necessarily rejected *per se*. Information, however, is a powerful force multiplier and the media is controlled by a few big corporations, with many of them located in America. Little known to many people, media corporations can make us perceive the world "not as it is," but "as they present it to us." (29)

In this vein, I will never forget my first experience in America from an information point of view. A daily newspaper in my native Romania was 4 pages in the 1960s and occasionally 6 or 8 pages. The *New York Times*, Sunday edition, was some 200 pages. Who could read it? The conclusion was clear. One can mislead with lack of information as well as with over-information; in other words through omission or commission. In spite of the overabundance of information, the average American can be informed or remain uninformed or misinformed. The English language media does all of them. One has to be very savvy to muddle through such a media and find the truth.

Many countries reject the "Americanization" of the world, but the trend continues to have profound popular appeal. Even in strictly traditional countries where some American programs are banned, many officials indulge in savoring them behind closed doors. However, some countries have reacted strongly against American cultural influences. France, for example, is trying to protect its language by imposing quotas on American films and television programs; Iran has banned the satellite dishes; and China is trying to control the internet. Actually, according to the

Associated Press of December 28, 2012, China began to require all users of the internet to register with the authorities.

Even here in the United States, some organizations want to censor heavy rock music and offensive lyrics which are prone to lead to violence. Often times, TV programs also use a very vulgar language and air decadent attitudes. Occasionally, such programs inspire barbaric behavior that afterwards is lamented in the same media. Truth is that American TV programs are omnipresent and transform people into consumers. Indeed, many programs are directed toward shaping people's desires according to the interests of the sponsors. And television has a huge impact on people because by 2000 as much as 98.8 percent of all American homes had at least one TV set. It has been estimated that an American watches 7 hours and 30 minutes of TV programs daily. As a direct result, most people want the things they see advertised on television. Even children as young as 3 years of age are made into consumers, and some of them have already developed their own favorite programs and brands. Parents cannot really control their children anymore since this is a universal trend, and because they also watch a lot of TV shows. (30)

What most people do not realize fully is that overwhelmingly TV programs are paid for by various sponsors who make money by promoting their goods and services. Accordingly, at prime time there are 15 minutes of ads for every hour of programming. And at the Super Bowl, the biggest sport event in the US, a 30-second commercial spot costs millions of dollars. Thus, whoever sponsors the ads, controls the media and influences our attitude, behavior and even our values.

Many people complain that television consumerism has become unethical and soulless. TV producers, however, complain that serious shows, educational programs, and even news broadcasts do not attract people and are not profitable. This is why some programs have been transformed into "gossip" or shallow entertainment shows to the detriment of real journalism. Fortunately, there are thousands of TV channels in the US, and the serious viewer can still sift through and find something good and suitable to his or her taste and interest. Yet, average citizens remain largely uninformed about the world.

Should governments get involved in the media industry? Or should they let the industry regulate itself? Media industry claims that it is not in business to promote education; it is in business to make money. Please, remember again that media means information and information is power. And yes, people do not perceive the world "as it is," but as the media "is presenting it to us." And our behavior, attitude and values are shaped by our perceptions . . .

THE GOVERNMENT AND THE ENVIRONMENT

The state of the natural environment is also a bone of contention between big businesses pushing for more globalization and governments which want to safeguard a healthier environment. The reality is that ecological problems are international and sometimes global. Air and water pollution, for example, know no borders; the oceans are open bodies of water; and the ozone layer is global. For example, many debris and even entire boats dislodged by the 2011 tsunami off the coast of

Japan ended up across the ocean in the Northwest US. Can the states of Washington or Oregon sue Japan for such ecological consequences? They may, but only national governments and international agencies can cope with such problems, and they are deeply divided. So far only big corporations have business plans at a global level, and the state of the environment is low on their agendas. At the same time, international organizations have limited power and national governments often pursue selfish goals. The result is that people and local communities are many times left to fend for themselves.

Attitudes toward the environment differ and reflect local culture and interests. Generally, for the Western world, man is the master of the environment and nature is a resource to be transformed into various goods. However, excessive demands for material goods have resulted in grave ecological deteriorations. In addition, huge accidents have caused immense damages and unacceptable loss of life. Here are a few examples well researched in *Wikipedia*:

* The Bhopal accident that occurred at a Union Carbide factory in 1984 in India caused about 8,000 deaths. Most people died during the following two weeks. However, according to the official report of the Indian government the accident affected about half a million people.

* The Chernobyl nuclear disaster that occurred in 1986 in Ukraine caused about 4,000 deaths, exposed hundreds of thousands of people to excessive radiation, and reached a vast area from Scandinavia to southern Europe.

* The Exxon Valdez tanker accident of 1989 spilled between 260,000 and 750,000 barrels of oil that covered 1,300 miles of the Alaskan coastline. The skipper of the ship was drunk, but with Exxon's high connections intervening for the company, the authorities were not allowed to check the level of alcohol in his blood till 24 hours later.

* The Gulf of Mexico oil drilling accident of April 2010 at a rig owned by British Petroleum caused a number of deaths and a huge environmental damage. The lawsuit that followed revealed the intricate links between owners and insurers and the difficulties for the authorities to pinpoint exactly the culprits. Yet, with the best lawyers and high-level political connections TNCs are getting away with murder.

Generally speaking, current ecological trends are discouraging and the leading causes among them are: overuse of non-renewable resources, continuous deforestation, depletion of water resources, destruction of local eco-systems, and others. These causes lead to air and water pollution, soil degradation, and health problems including death. Some of the most visible human-induced effects are: acid rain caused by emissions of sulfuric oxide combined with water, greenhouse effects caused by excessive emissions of carbon dioxide, and climate changes. From a climatic stand point, the scientists are rather divided. In the past, leftist circles insisted on "global warming" caused primarily by excessive human activities. However, by being unable to prove it, the same circles have changed their tune and now they call it climate change. Globalists on the other hand claim that warming up and cooling off are natural cycles of the earth and thus, not much can be done. Both theories have some truth in them, but the reality is that current environmental problems continue and they represent a danger to our civilization.

In the United States, the chief watch dog of the environment is the Environmental Protection Agency (EPA). In this regard, and in order to keep a healthy ecological balance, governments must work with TNCs, with local communities, and with various non-governmental organizations (NGO). And to address successfully many ecological problems it takes determination, money and compromises. Yet, it is hard to have a piece of cake and to eat it too! Should governments exercise strict controls and set up rigid regulations and safety measures? Or should they let the big corporations take care of the matter? Remember that stringent environmental rules endanger economic development and employment. Lax environmental rules endanger the eco-systems and threaten life itself. No international corporation is willing to address this dilemma. Thus, only governments, representing the will of the people, are legitimately entrusted and morally obligated to find a solution to our environmental problems.

China again, as the new powerhouse of the world, offers a good case study. Hundreds of millions of Chinese have moved to cities in recent decades for jobs and for higher standards of living. Such mass migrations helped decrease the pressure on the rural land, but it also caused environmental problems. According to the *Economist* of December 15, 2012, the capital city of Beijing and its surroundings have bypassed 20 million inhabitants. As a result, the city is heavily polluted, the auto traffic is impossible, and there is already a big shortage of fresh water. Under such conditions, some leaders even recommend building a new capital in the central part of the country. Shanghai, on the other hand, became a city of 23 million, which exceeds the entire population of Australia. The population increase and the resultant environmental problems reflected Chairman Mao's position during the first years of his regime. He claimed that each person comes with two hands, therefore must work, and to increase the food production he launched the slogan "man must conquer nature." Consequently, millions of trees were cut down to make room for agriculture, but instead of better crops, the process caused floods and ecological disasters. At some point, billions of small birds were also killed because allegedly they would eat part of the crop, but the result was catastrophic. Without birds, insects multiplied exponentially and they ate the roots of the plants. As a consequence, big swathes of land were degraded, some soils died, and crops failed.

From an industrial point of view, the Chinese development is mostly powered by burning coal, which is also overwhelmingly used for home heating and for cooking. But overreliance on coal for energy creates huge environmental problems. It has been calculated, for example, that 25 percent of the air pollution in Los Angeles, California, is caused by the coal burning in China. And there is not much that can be done. China is the world's biggest producer of coal and at the same time, the world's biggest importer of coal. According to *Los Angeles Times* of 26 August 2012, to satisfy its ever increasing energy needs, China already uses half of the world coal production. And the need for coal will be even greater in the future if China continues its current industrial development.

The recent increasing use of oil by the growing number of auto vehicles in China is not an encouraging trend either. From this point of view, imagine a world whereby China has adopted the American life style. According to the article "Passenger cars per 1,000 People," available on *Google* research, in 2009 there were 450 cars per thousand people in the United States and only 34 per thousand in China. Imagine 500 million cars in China! What will their economic and ecological effects be locally and globally? And yet, who has the right to deny the Chinese people the right of owning an automobile? Recently, China has become the biggest car producer in the world!

10 — Globalization Marches on

To be successful in today's world, a corporation must find a specific niche and explore and exploit it to the fullest. In a way, it is the biological survival of the fittest. Patrick Buchanan even compares global corporations with big sharks which naturally must swim and look for food continuously. If they stop, they die! (31) Humans are more than biological beings, but in order to survive, corporations must combine human aspirations with ruthless biological traits. It is an uneasy balance between corporate interests, national governments, the greed of the few, and the needs of the many. The next pages focus on several important industries. For an in-depth study, see among others *Global Shift* by Peter Dicken. The 600-page book provides a multitude of details and case studies as well as many graphs and illustrations.

Anthropologically, in order to survive people need food, clothes, and shelter. Historically, these basic necessities were obtained from the local environment, and they mirrored the nature surrounding early man. There were huge differences between the food available in the tropics and the clothes people needed there and the food found in an Arctic environment and the clothes necessary to survive in the frigid cold. Also, there was nothing in common between an American Indian adobe, for example, and an Inuit igloo. Yet, modern cities from Amazonia to Siberia look alike today, youngsters all over the world want to wear Levis, and many food items are very much globalized. The process of globalization has brought about many changes, more uniformity, and a certain reordering of priorities. Thus, it seems that modern man has altered the very natural order of basic needs. In fact, the distinction between *what we need* and *what we want* is getting increasingly blurred. Thus, modern man everywhere needs food, clothes . . . and automobiles to get around. Who does not want a car? But, before we take the driver's seat, we need to clothe ourselves and get a quick bite.

FOOD AND THE AGRO-BUSINESS INDUSTRY

Food is the most basic human need! Yet, during the last several decades food has become a global business representing not only nutrition, but also a sign of new life-style. As nutrition, basic food needs are meats, fruits and vegetable, but many people are looking now for "high-value" or "organic" food. At the same time, what we consume depends on taste, upbringing and culture, education, religion, health, ethical attitude and disposable income. Some of these factors are more stable while others may change with the passing of time.

From a monetary point of view, if some 50 years ago the cost of food in the Western countries accounted for about 30 percent of average incomes, now this cost has been reduced to only 10 percent of incomes. In Europe, for example, according to a study published by *Romania Libera* on 29 August 2012, England pays the least for its food, about 10 percent of average incomes, while Romania pays 30 percent, which is the highest in Europe. Generally, in the developing countries the cost of food accounts for a larger proportion of family incomes. Nevertheless, there is much more food available today everywhere in the world than 50 years ago. The problem is how to afford it.

Sadly, from another point of view, many people continue to starve while a lot of food is wasted. According to the article "Food Waste in America," published by the Society of St. Andrew and available on *Google* research, in the United States 40 percent of all food is wasted. Several studies have concluded that some crops are left in the fields because of inadequate harvests, some food is discarded by supermarkets, and a good part is discarded at home. Worst still, some food is also destroyed on purpose to keep the prices high. All these create another undesirable dichotomy in the era of globalization. Many persons in the advanced countries suffer now of obesity and related health problems, while a lot of people in the poor countries continue to starve. And even if there is plenty of food available in some parts of the world, the cost of transportation is too steep to send it where it is needed. The conclusion is that in a world of plenty, some people continue to starve. "Water, water is everywhere, but not a drop to drink!"

Current food cornucopia has been achieved through the so-called Green Revolution, and through Biotechnology and Genetics. The Green Revolution increased dramatically the production of wheat, rice and maize by using new seeds, better fertilizers, pesticides and herbicides, as well as modern irrigation systems and new farming techniques. The application of science in agriculture also led to new plant and animal feeds that accelerate growth. In this regard it is interesting to visit any American State Fairs in the fall to see with amazement the individual achievements of many farmers. In the fall of 2012, as reported by the *Arizona Daily Star* of 9 October 2012, the record for a traditional American pumpkin was 1,775 pounds. That is a humongous 810 kilos!

On the negative side, modern agricultural methods have led to risk-prone monocultures in some countries, to cultural clashes in others, and to resistance against genetically modified new forms of life. Genetic alterations, for example, were needed for increased productions, cost considerations, resistance to transportation, extended shelf-life, and easier retailing. In some cases, certain plants varieties, such as tomatoes, have been altered to precise specifications.

In addition, in order to reach the consumers in marketable conditions, many fruits and vegetables must be harvested green and allowed to ripen on the way. And to keep them fresh and to look attractive, specialists use thousands of chemical substances. Such new varieties are less expensive, but they are also often odorless and almost tasteless. Personally, it took me several years in the United States to get adjusted to the taste of tomatoes and grapes, among others. Sadly, many Western food items leave a lot to be desired. Abundance also came with dubious quality. Furthermore, it has been calculated that 40 percent of the total cost of food paid by a customer in a modern supermarket is just for packaging. In today's world it seems that "looking good" is as important as "being good." And this also applies to food.

Modern agro-business has also developed expensive "designer" foods such as Starbucks coffee. Coffee is highly consumed in the United States and is a 75 billion dollar annual global business. Coffee, by the way, originated in Ethiopia, where I visited several farms, but now it grows better in South America. The plant comes in two basic varieties: *Arabica*, which is more demanding and more expensive and grows at higher altitudes, and *Robusta*, which is less expensive and grows at lower altitudes in the humid tropics. Currently, Brazil produces 30 percent of world coffee and is the world's biggest producer. Allegedly, coffee was smuggled into Brazil and it is said that the huge production of today started with one single plant brought from the Caribbean islands.

Food production continues to be locally based and depends on soil and climate, but agro-businesses are international. However, food consumption is now global and big corporations aspire to create "global" brands and to conquer the entire world with them. At the same time, seasonality is gone in the developed countries. For affluent consumers it is "spring and summer" all the time. In this vein, there is a complementary relationship between North and South, especially between North and South America. For examples, during the winter, the United States imports grapes from Chile. Generally, however, the rich countries of the northern hemisphere import fresh food from the south year-round. On the negative side, this relationship can destroy the local producers. Recently, for example, there was a "tomatoes war" between the Florida growers and the Mexican growers who managed to out-compete the American farmers.

Modern agriculture is a far cry from the traditional subsistence farming, and the local and small family farms may soon become a relic of the past. They are being replaced by big agro-businesses. Agro-businesses, however, require huge capital investments, good organization, effective transportation, and very good marketing, distribution, and retailing. All these factors force final prices to go up and to become rather universal. For example, while visiting a commercial pineapple farm in Hawaii, I was surprised to find out that local prices were similar to New York prices. Why were the prices so high when retailers did not have to add the cost of packaging and transportation? As a matter of fact, transporting fresh produce is expensive and essential because most items are fragile and perishable and require a controlled atmosphere. Anyway, food production and processing is no longer simple agriculture; it is very much science and technology.

The American company Tyson Foods, for example, is the biggest poultry company in the world and somehow a world onto itself. The company works with many local people helping them to build chicken coops and providing them with one-day old chicks and the necessary feed. Then, after a few weeks, the company trucks come around and collect the chicken for the slaughterhouse. Everything is calculated with precision so that the chicken should be fully grown and should command the best price. If collected a few days later the chickens "eat up" the company profit. If collected a few days before they are fully grown, they bring less profit. The situation is similar with turkeys, pigs, and cattle, animals that can grow crammed up together in their enclosures. Strangely, sheep refuse to be regimented and they only prosper in open fields. This is probably why most lamb consumed in the United States comes from Australia and New Zealand.

Interestingly, lamb is highly consumed in southern Europe, especially in the spring, but to be marketed as lamb the animal must be just a few weeks old. In Australia, the government classifies the slaughtered animal as lamb if it is under six months old. Yet, the same government allows lamb to be exported to Europe as long as the slaughtered animal is under one year of age. The reality is that each species has a specific growing time and slaughtering them before the full potential growth is reached is counterproductive. And of course the quality of the meat depends on the age of the slaughtered animal, as well as on the feed it consumed. If in a poor country animals are raised traditionally, modern farm animals are raised scientifically under the supervision of many specialists.

The role of the government in agriculture and the food industry is delicate and very important. Almost regardless of the cost, the government must help the farmers and the national agriculture, and at the same time, must protect the consumer. In this regard, governments keep the process going through specific policies and with safety regulations. In the United States the chief authorities are the US Department of Agriculture (USDA, alias Uncle Sam) and the Food and Drug Administration (FDA). They apply the rules and regulations, check the process, and occasionally fine the culprits.

The government also encourages and subsidizes agricultural research as it did in the poultry industry. Yet, during the last decades of the 20th Century some people tried hard to establish a new farming branch-emu growing. Emus are little demanding ostrich-like birds native to Australia that subsist on marginal and dry lands. Their meat is tasty, similar to beef, and their eggs are edible. The American supermarkets, however, are satiated with all sorts of meats and have little room for more products. On the other hand, the government did not find it necessary to invest in the research in order to transform the small-scale production into an assembly-line agro-industry. At the same time, large butcher houses refused to process the new birds unless the farmers provided them with huge numbers to justify their operations. It was a vicious circle and in the end the new trend lost its allure. What a pity! I visited several such little farms and the emu meat was indeed very good.

At the dawn of the new millennium, modern agro-business is rapidly getting globalized. If fifty years ago 90 percent of all food was locally produced and consumed, currently, some countries import 90 percent of their foods. Actually, despite having good agricultural resources, many countries import food now from abroad rather than producing their own. In this situation, agricultural negotiations between countries are often acrimonious. Japan, for example, refuses to open its rice market although foreign rice is considerably less expensive. The United States subsidizes its milk industry and refuses to open America to less expensive imports. In fact, many national governments protect their agricultural sector and subsidize heavily some produce. The European Union subsidizes each cow with about 2 dollars per day. Also, EU farmers export wheat at 28 percent less than it costs to produce, rice at 25 percent less, and corn at 10 percent less. (32) Indeed, many countries cannot afford to alienate their farmers. According to the *Economist* of November 24, 2012, the European Union spends 40 percent of its budget on agriculture, while agriculture generates only 2 percent of the

EU gross domestic product and employs less than 5 percent of the workforce.

As for the agro-business, all this time, big corporations lobby governments for protection when needed, for open markets when convenient, and for more globalization when beneficial to themselves. Big corporations also tend to monopolize all agricultural stages from seed production, to planting, growing, harvesting, processing and distribution. As a consequence, a few huge corporations dominate the world.

Nestle, a giant Swiss company, is the world's largest food conglomerate marketing about 8,000 brands and 20,000 varieties. Recently, Nestle recruited a local Brazilian distributor in Sao Paulo and began to offer its products door-to-door and even on credit to the remotest corners of the country. According to the *Economist* of December 15, 2012, Nestle has even acquired a boat that cruises the Amazon River offering local inhabitants packaged food and ice cream. The company is looking indeed for any nook and cranny to expand its empire and to conquer the entire world. Yet, some local health advocates became very angry, insisting that such food is not safe and healthy. Such complains do not stop the expansion. Whenever needed, Nestle adjusts its products to local taste. For example, observing that the Chinese do not like the bitter taste of coffee, Nestle has patented for them a sugary coffee-based drink that tastes like ice cream. And the new product sells well in China.

The first MacDonald restaurant. San Bernardino, California, 1940.

Source: Wikipedia

Other examples of food companies going global are offered by the fizzy drinks and by the expansion of chain restaurants. The above mentioned source shows that the marketing of soft drinks has increased tremendously in recent decades and has acquired true global proportions. Presently, Coca Cola and Pepsi Cola control 40 percent of all soft drinks marketed globally and are available virtually everywhere. No wonder some people complain against the "cocalization" of the world. As for chain-food restaurants, McDonald for example, headquartered now in Oak Brook, Illinois, is present currently with some 33,000 establishments in 119 countries around the globe. And the trend is to expand even further continues.

Problem is that when such giants penetrate a local market the local producers, stores and vendors are often annihilated.

Occasionally, even local food brands are taken over by international corporations, repackaged, and registered in their names. I was surprised when visiting my native country to discover that the traditional Romanian borsht made of wheat bran was remade into a powder, packaged to international standards, and marketed by a Spanish company. The result is that smaller grocers and retailers are ruthlessly out-competed and replaced by giant companies such as Walmart, Carrefour, Metro, or Tesco. In a way these international food companies and retailers tell us what to eat.

Who is a winner and who is a loser in the globalization of the food industry? The answer is simple: Whoever has the money. There is no question that food is more plentiful and more available, but food processing and marketing allow the big corporations to impose rather uniform global prices. That means that such food is outside the reach of many people. A Starbucks coffee, for example, made from good Ethiopian coffee bought for little money, may cost 5 dollars a cup. Can a poor farmer afford it? Starbucks is a global brand name now. It offers good coffee and it attracts upper middle class people to sip the tasty brand, to socialize, and to even show off their outfits. And this takes us to the garment industry.

THE GARMENT INDUSTRY

Clothing is also a quasi-essential human need. Clothes protect the body, but also embellish it. While visiting southern Ethiopia, where I was a professor for two years, I was surprised to see in more remote places of the country naked men and semi-naked women. Some of the women were covered up in what I considered ornaments rather that real clothes, which convinced me that clothes are not necessarily essential for human survival.

Historically, clothing responds to biological, social, and cultural forces, but also helps people express themselves. As symbols, clothes suggest self-perception and self-projection. And yet, beyond basic necessities, with increasing incomes, people aspire for attractive fashion garments. Thus, the modern trend in this field is from strict necessity to fashion and even to luxurious clothes. Accordingly, current demand for clothing is 45 percent basic, 27 percent for basic fashion, and 28 percent for luxury items. Global corporations follow this trend and adjust their production and marketing as necessary to satisfy local needs, taste and personal purses. (33) In the process, known brand names make fortunes. *Time* magazine of November 5, 2012 reported, for example, that in 2011 the footwear companies Nike and Adidas respectively made 8.7 and 7 billion dollars in international sales.

The clothing industry is labor intensive because many operations cannot be mechanized. For example, sewing and assembling account for 80 percent of all labor cost. Yet, this makes decentralization and subcontracting work possible. Indeed, sweat shops are now located throughout the world, especially in the developing countries, where as a rule they employ young and little skilled women. Otherwise, with an ever growing demand for clothing by an ever growing population, the garment industry is highly globalized. However, the links between designing, producing, advertising and marketing are flexible and complex. The designing, for example, could be done in such cosmopolitan centers as New York and Paris, while the sewing and assembling is done anywhere from Mexico to Indonesia. Eventually, the end products are shipped wherever in demand for sales.

In the United States, the most important garment retailers are department stores, discount stores, factory outlets, fashion-oriented stores, and specialized boutiques. Examples of big department stores are Sears, J.C. Penney, Macy's and others. As for fashion stores, if one visits Las Vegas for example, he or she will be impressed by the number of elegant stores and also by their prices: Christian Dior, Polo-Ralph Lauren, Armani, Benetton, Hugo Boss, Luis Vuitton, Jimmy Choo, Coco Channel, etc. Interestingly, most garment companies are now international to the point that they belong to a country only in name. The very American Levi Strauss, for example, has all its production now overseas.

As for the quality of clothing, it is a matter of interpretation and dispute. Some well-known brand names do offer items of good quality. Others, however, strive on the prestige of the name. Nevertheless, wearing the label regardless of quality is overwhelmingly important for some snobs. A pair of women shoes can costs one thousand dollars. A man's shirt and tie could cost one hundred dollars. But if such fashion stores do not sell their merchandise, they send them to low-end stores where they are sold for a fraction of the original price. It is true that sometimes the inside labels are torn, but do people wear labels or items of clothing? Answering this question should place respondents in their rightful social category! Sadly, the recent polarization of the world has filled many cities with luxury stores while many people live in poverty. A case in point is Bucharest, the capital of Romania.

The newspaper of wide circulation *Romania Libera* of 13 December 2012 published an article announcing the opening of a new luxury store belonging to the Italian designer Roberto Cavalli. According to the paper, the store will be located in the five-star hotel Marriott-Bucharest alongside the Alfred Dunhill, Valentino, Ermanno, Scervino and Escada boutiques. As prices, a Cavalli dress will cost between 600 and 15,000 dollars and a woman's bag will cost between 1,200 and 5,000 dollars. There is no question that some people will be able to afford the new luxury items. However, it should be kept in mind that average salaries in Romania are about 300 dollars per month and many retired people, and there are a lot of them, have half that monthly income. Yet, prices are similar, and in some cases even higher, than in the United States. How do people survive? Many families have close relatives who work abroad and send home remittances. And the government keeps borrowing irresponsibly from international bankers.

On the positive side, the globalization of the garment industry is producing more clothes than ever before, thus dressing up the entire world and satisfying all tastes and needs. Virtually, no one has to walk around barefoot or clad in rags anymore these days and many people are actually looking elegant all over the world. By the turn of the 19th Century, one could recognize the wealthy by the clothes they wore. These days, most average persons are well-dressed while the rich wear casual clothes. "Clothes do not make a man" anymore, at least in regular settings. Yet, when the super wealthy socialize among themselves, they no longer wear clothes, they wear labels.

On the negative side, while big TNCs operating in poor countries do provide local employment opportunities, very often employees work in sordid conditions for minimum wages and almost without any rights. Many times, such industries hire, use and abuse vulnerable women, children, and convicts. Working conditions can also be unbearable causing accidents and victims. As recently as November 26, 2012, the *Associated Press* reported that a fire at a garment factory in Bangladesh, which worked for Walmart, killed at least 12 persons. Then, on December 13 *Bloomberg News* announced that such incidents occur on a regular basis. Yet, local authorities and even national governments cannot really control the industry because of its fragmentation and because often times responsible officials work in collusion with the garment corporations. People who work in such factories do manage to eke out a living, but the big corporations make fortunes and drive social polarization even further. Nevertheless, in a world of globalization many nicely dressed people walk around to show off their clothes, while others drive proudly in their newly acquired cars. They have joined the global world.

11 — The Automobile Industry, Energy and Other Needs of Modern Humanity

For about one century, the automobile industry was considered "the industry of industries" and was associated with economic strength and national pride. America was the pioneer in the field, and Detroit, with hundreds of car factories in the past, was the automobile capital of the world. America was also the first country to offer personal mobility and status to everybody. Here are a few landmarks of the industry.

The auto industry was revolutionized by Henry Ford who invented the assembly line. As a result, mass production replaced individual and artisan work, and workers became sort of cogs serving the assembly lines. Working at an assembly line is not easy, but most people manning them manage the necessary tempo, do not have to be skilled, and make a decent living. Currently, car-making is essentially an assembly industry. Many companies have also installed robots in the process, and gradually, mass production has been replaced by flexible production. In this vein, the latest trend is replacing groups of pieces with "modules." This move has led to new relations between the main factory and a multitude of subcontractors that supply various parts or entire modules. Such subcontractors are now spread all over the world. The end result is that from "national" auto production became very much "international" and global.

Henry Ford, the inventor of the assembly line, circa 1919.
Source: Wikipedia

At a personal and family level, cars are probably the most coveted things in today's world. In the United States, buying a car represents the second highest investments after buying a house and for most people cars are necessities. It is common for many Americans, for example, to commute one hundred miles round trip every day between homes and places of work. The nature of America is such that large cities are sprawls, public transportation is inadequate, and distances are huge. There is no choice but the private car. Automobiles represent both necessities and luxuries at the same time. As a necessity cars are maintained for long use, but as luxury they are changed often "to keep up with the Joneses." In addition, cars also reflect self-image, social position, and personal life-style. (34)

Although no longer a unique symbol, the auto industry remains an important factor in today's global economy. The industry is also a force multiplier bringing along more employment and activities than almost any other industrial activity. Globally, according to the *Economist* of 4 September 2004, at the time the auto industry used 50 percent of all oil, 25 percent of all rubber, and 15 percent of all glass. In addition, the industry engages in many related services from banking and insurance to maintenance, bringing employment and profits to many other activities. Little wonder new car plants are being built all over the world. The American car companies, for example, have built factories in China; the German companies opened assembly lines in the United States; and so far Japan has built 15 assembly plants in the United States and Canada. Yet, through various acquisitions and mergers, automobile production is concentrated now in a few countries. This concentration reflects the buying power of the local markets, as in the United States, as well as the availability of local labor and materials to build cars, as in South Korea.

According to *Google,* in 2011 the world produced about 80 million vehicles of which 60 million were passenger cars. Surprisingly, China was the biggest producer with over 18 million cars, followed by the United States and Japan. Other big auto producers in 2011 and 2012 were Germany, France, South Korea and Spain. Together, these countries manufactured about 70 percent of all 2011 passenger cars. And according to *Financial Times* of January 2, 2013, China is expected to produce 19.6 million cars this year bypassing for the first time the entire car production of Europe, which also includes Russia and Turkey. Auto parts for assembly lines, however, come from all over the world. At the same time, the automobiles industry is fiercely competitive, remains a significant and prestigious industry and personal cars continue to be highly coveted.

As for social consequences, many corporations prosper and make big profits, especially by relocating production to low labor-cost countries. Such relocations or newly built factories bring employment to local workers, transfer some modern technologies, and increase local standards of living. China, for example, attracted many car producers in recent years and negotiated a number of mutually beneficial contracts. Foreign companies found ideal conditions in China, while the Chinese government created new employment opportunities for its multitude of workers. With new global awareness and with increasing auto production at home, nothing can prevent the Chinese from wanting their personal cars.

And since we have just focused on the automobile industry, everybody knows how important gas and oil is for moving things around. The globalization of energy, especially of the car fuel, is actually visible at almost every important city intersection. And the global search for new oil fields has led to many wars in the past and is still a *casus belli* these days. The first Gulf War in the 1990s and the recent Iraq War are only two such examples. And while the Western companies are trying hard to establish themselves in the Caspian-South Asia oil fields, the Russians are penetrating the European markets, and the Chinese are searching worldwide for new sources.

Oil or petroleum in Latin (meaning stone oil) is a commodity indispensable now to our modern civilization. Scarcely anything could move without it. As a consequence, the oil industry, from exploration to extraction, and from refining and transportation around the world to retailing stations at the corner of our streets, is one of the most globalized economic activities. Oil has been known and used since antiquity, but it was the invention of the internal combustion engine that put it on wheels and transformed it from a gluey substance into the black gold of today. Ever since, automobiles and oil have gone hand-in-hand.

Unfortunately, as a resource, oil is unevenly and unfairly spread around the globe. Some big countries, notably Russia, the United States, and Canada, are endowed with huge oil reserves. Some very small countries, like Kuwait, Bahrain, the United Arab Emirates and others, are also blessed with huge reserves. Such small countries have achieved true economic miracles based upon their oil sources. There are, however, also countries that squander their oil reserves to enrich ruthless politicians with no benefits for their population.

Oil is a non-renewable energy source which, according to some specialists, has already peaked at its maximum production capacity at a global level. If other fields are not discovered, from now on oil production is expected to decline. That makes some world leaders worry and compel responsible people to look for alternative sources of energy. Yet, the perspectives so far are little encouraging. While the reserves are limited, the needs for oil and gas are insatiable. Could the world sustain an ever increasing population and a never ending demand for fuel? This is indeed a big question.

Currently, the biggest producers of oil are Saudi Arabia, Russia and the United States. At the same time, the United States, China, Japan and Europe are the biggest importers and consumers of oil. In North America, Mexico and Canada are also big oil producers and they export the surplus to the United States. In Europe, the biggest producers are Norway and Great Britain. Interestingly, in 1900 Romania was the biggest producer of oil in Europe, but by 2000 Romanian production decreased from a peak of over 14 million tons to about 4-5 million tons.

Burj Khalifa, Dubai, UAE, World's tallest building erected
with petro-dollars. Source: Wikipedia

In 1960 some of the biggest producers formed a special
cartel, the Organization of Petroleum Exporting Countries
(OPEC), in order to better control the supply and the price of
oil on the global markets. The organization is headquartered in

Vienna and does manage to influence the market to a certain degree, but the price of gas is also controlled by the international oil corporations and by the big banks that facilitate their operations. Often times, for example, when the price per barrel at extraction grows by 10 percent, big corporations like Exxon Mobile increase the price of gas at the pump by 30 percent. Such companies make huge profits. Yet, with ever increasing demands it is possible that in the future from a plain commodity, oil might become a luxury item. Then, the car owners will stand out as wealthy people.

The globalization fever has caught up with virtually every aspect of modern economic activity. The media industry, as another example, tends to become increasingly global. CNN News has evolved from an American attempt to focus on news into an international TV program threatening the well-established BBC News. Also, the Arab broadcasting company Al Jazeera (The Island in Arabic) rose from an unknown entity to international prominence competing successfully with the other two giants. National Geographic, initially a printed magazine, is now a very well established global media brand. Publishing, especially in English, is also a global business now.

One of the most important fields of globalization is the international financial system that is backing every aspect of the process. International financial activities are essential in today's global operations. Practically no economic transaction can take place without financial arrangements. At the same time, "plastic cards" instead of money and information about money rather than real money, are travelling now non-stop globally and instantly. As a result, financial institutions are currently located around the globe. Furthermore, new financial services have diversified tremendously and are offering a vast array of services. Under these conditions, trust is of the essence in today's world, but trust is also abused by modern swindlers. And crooks cheat people and institutions of billions of dollars in a globalized world. With a multitude of bogus financial institutions mushrooming over night all over the globe, it is harder and harder for traditional institutions to operate and for authorities to monitor them.

The most important financial centers in the world today are London followed by New York and Tokyo. There are 470 foreign banks in London by comparison with 320 in Frankfurt and 214 in Paris. At the same time, many financial centers have been relocated "offshore" in order to avoid national jurisdictions. Such operations are generally tax havens and booking centers. For example, there are about 300,000 foreign financial centers in the Virgin Islands, although only 9,000 of them have any activity there. There are also 500 such companies in the Cayman Islands, but only 70 have physical locations there. Such centers operate legally, but at the limit of the law. The result is that financial activities are increasingly difficult to follow and to control and that leads to serious problems. (35)

The chief problems caused by the globalization of finances are laundering dirty money from drug trafficking, speculative profits, and other dubious activities. Drug trafficking is probably the worst disease of our increasingly globalized world. It represents a frightening epidemic and tragically is one of the most lucrative businesses in today's world. Interpol, regular police, and other law-enforcement agencies try to follow the traffickers and the financial swindlers, but often times their cases fall through the cracks in the complicated financial world of today. And when eventually some crooks are caught, they benefit from the best lawyers money can buy and often get away with minimum punishments.

With regard to the international financial institutions, sadly, some reputable banks are also involved in dirty deals these days. On December 13, 2012, for example, the *Associated Press* reported that the giant Swiss bank UBS AG of Zurich admitted to US, British, and Swiss authorities to having been involved in a huge fraud. Accordingly, the bank agreed to compensate them to the tune of 1.5 billion dollars. How many others allegedly honorable banks have done the same thing without being caught? Such criminal activities give some kind of legitimacy to the shady international financial transactions.

Money! Money! Money! Greed! Greed! Greed! Indeed, for some speculators globalization is all about money. Some people swindle hundreds of millions. The American investor Bernard Madoff cheated his clients of 20 billion dollars. Other criminals kill for a few dollars. Both these groups have sold their souls for the money. And while the Wall Street swindlers pushed America to the brink of financial collapse in 2008, street thugs are making Main Street America unsafe for the decent citizen. To a good degree, they all act with impunity because these days the world is controlled by minorities. In the case of financial globalization the world is manipulated, used, and abused by a moneyed minority with global reach. Big bankers at the top, petty criminals at the bottom, and Mafiosi in the middle! Long live the new world!

12 — Is Globalization Good or Bad?

There is presently a growing interest in globalization studies and the process has already triggered strong positive and negative reactions. Globalization is strongly supported by TNCs, by the powerful countries, by many international organizations, and by a handful of individuals who stand to benefit from it. However, there is also strong opposition to globalization. The strongest pro-globalization group is made up of the so-called "Market Globalists." The anti-globalization movement is made up chiefly of two large categories: "Justice Globalists" and "Nationalists or Patriots."

Market globalists advocate free and unrestricted international trade and venerate consumerism as a new religion. As a rule, such supporters are secular or atheistic (actually many of them hate God and religion) and they also abhor the nation-state. For them, the traditional state is an artificial and temporary arrangement that needs to be dismantled. Globalists are also supported by secret and semi-secret organizations and by big business publications such as *The Economist, Wall Street Journal, Financial Times, Business Week,* and others.

In order to justify their position, market globalists claim that globalization is inevitable and irreversible; that no one is in charge of the process; that there is no hidden agenda; and, thus, there is no conspiracy behind globalization to speak of. Furthermore, they claim that globalization spreads democracy throughout the world and brings benefits to everyone. About this point, they admit that if not everybody is benefiting now, they will benefit in the future. (The communists also promised future abundance to everybody, but as some students used to joke, that abundance was to come in another geological era.)

Globalists also insist on "a self-regulating market" that should serve as "the framework for a future global order." (36) Indeed, *Business Week* of 13 December 1999 claimed that *"Globalization is the triumph of markets over governments."* Yet, globalists need the help of the governments to attain their goals and to advance their agendas. Question is, if globalization is natural or irreversible and people have no choice and nothing to say about it, where is the freedom of choice? Where is the democracy that globalization is supposed to bring about?

It should be pointed out that the United States is a determined advocate of globalization and that a large number of American TNCs have taken advantage of the process. But not everybody in the United States has benefitted. In reality, there is strong opposition among many Americans.

Justice Globalists and their mostly leftists "social justice movement" oppose the process and stress among other things the disparities and social polarization caused by globalization. This group includes environmentalists, humanists, some religious activists, liberal academics and others who advocate radical changes. Unfortunately, such people are trying to combine two incompatible trends: old democratic traditions with new countercultural values of the New Age, such as moral relativism. In fact, the entire ideology of globalization is an artificial hybrid between tolerant Western values, recent Western countercultural values, and old Marxist ideals masquerading now as libertarian or social-democratic. These diverging trends do not mix.

In his concise book, *Globalization*, Manfred Steger mentions the most important suggestions of this mixed bag of advocates. They are: a Global New Deal based on redistribution of wealth and power; a new global "Marshall Plan" to help the poor countries; forgiveness of all Third World debt; abolition of off-shore financial centers; establishing international labor protection standards; and greater transparency and accountability. (37) These are beautiful ideals, but will big business ever accept them? Besides, they are utopian dreams.

In 2000 representatives of justice globalism established the World Social Forum (WSF) to oppose the World Economic Forum (WEF), which met the same year in Davos, Switzerland, and which pushes for more globalization. David Rothkopf, author of the volume *Superclass,* attended that meeting and coined the participants as "Davos men." He described the participants, some of the richest and most powerful men in the world, not necessarily in the best of colors.

As for social consequences, some members of the World Social Forum *"fear that the aim of the globalists is to eventually eliminate the people who are not useful to the powerful."* (38) The reality is that the goal of most of the rich and powerful people has always been to give those who they need just about enough to let them survive. This was the rule in antiquity and during the Middle Ages. Why should the new super class of today help those who are not useful from their point of view? The thoughtful answer should be: to avoid the bloody revolts that occurred periodically throughout history; therefore, for their own good! Apparently, they do not listen. Yet, history teaches mankind something in this vein. Poor people do not revolt against the rich establishment out of envy; actually, many of them try to emulate the upper class. Poor people revolt out of desperation when they cannot make ends meet anymore. And this is the danger.

For the justice globalists, globalization is evil because it enriches a small minority and it impoverishes the majority. Therefore, from their point of view, the process must be stopped or controlled. Recently, these social justice groups began to organize big rallies against globalization. In December 1999, for example, they organized a rally against the meeting of the World Trade Organization held in Seattle. However, their demonstrations were met with hostility and even with brutality by the local authorities. No one gives up power and privilege voluntarily. There is "nothing new under the sun." It also happened in the past . . . until one day everything changed.

In the United States the anti-globalist movement is represented, among others, by the consumer advocate Ralph Nader and by the Human Rights activist and renowned linguist Noam Chomsky. Among the active anti-globalization organizations are Oxfam, Greenpeace, Friends of the Earth, as well as many other humanitarian and environmental groups. However, the world is fast becoming an increasingly open economic system and neither the political left nor the political right have an alternative or a practical solution. And this takes us to the political right, the nationalists and patriots, who also oppose globalization.

Nationalists or Patriots, as the nationalists are known in the United States, also oppose globalization and seek to preserve the nation-state and its prerogatives. As a rule, such people believe in God and advocate respect for national traditions. In support of their position, they quote historic personalities, such as the French thinker Ernest Renan, who wrote that *"a nation is a living soul"* and cannot be replaced with anything. Pat Buchanan also stressed that free trade cannot be a substitute for a nation, that *"an economy is not a country"* and that *"trade is not an end, but it is the means to an end."* (39) And the end should be helping the people and the nation survive and prosper.

Most American patriots insist on rebuilding the country around the old traditional values. In support of their stand, they invoke the Constitution, the prescribed role of the government, and the Declaration of Independence. *"We hold these truths to be self-evident, that all men are created equal, that they are endowed by the Creator with certain unalienable rights; that among these are Life, Liberty and the pursuit of Happiness . . ."* And the patriots remind us that the founding fathers decided to have a government *of the people, by the people, and for the people* . . . Many Americans are asking themselves, is this still true today? On the other hand, do globalists adhere to these principles? Hell no! They are prone to abandon them and to have them replaced with a yet to be known international agenda. American patriots like Pat Buchanan, a known journalist and writer, former presidential candidate, and adviser to President Reagan, insists to *"put America first."* He and others like him are against completely "free trade" because that ideal is utopia, meaning nowhere in Greek. In this vein he wrote:

"Global free trade is a Faustian bargain. A nation sells its soul for a cornucopia of foreign goods. First, the nation gives up its independence; then its sovereignty; and finally, its birthright—nationhood itself." And further he wrote: *"when the economic levers go, the political independence is sure to follow."* (40)

Many other patriots have also stressed that people are not just producers and consumers. *"They are members of a nation, with history, traditions, language, faith, culture and institutions to maintain and pass on."* (41) In the same vein, sociologist and philosopher Christian Kopff wrote about the subject and asked rhetorically: *"What doth it profit a man if he gains the whole world and suffers the loss of his country?"* (42) This is true about many countries!

Economically, the American patriots want to preserve the manufacturing industries as a guarantee for prosperity, sovereignty and independence. They point out that America is still strong, but current trends are alarming. And many of them warn that nations have failed in the past. And why do nations fail? Here are some reasons: corrupt and weak governments; hidden interests; abusive leaders; repressive regimes; lack of economic opportunities; instability and insecurity; uneducated or complacent population . . . (43)

Is the United States going this way? Is this the future of the world?

CONCLUDING REMARKS

This brief study has posed and analyzed a number of questions, but it did not answer directly the simple one: is globalization good or bad? Obviously, it is good for some and bad for many! It all depends on our social standing and on our conscience.

What's going on in the world? The "Thinking Man" of Hamangia, Romania.
Prehistoric statuette. Circa 4000 BC. Source: Google.Ro.

Globalization is only the economic arm of a new social philosophy in the making called "The New World Order," and we know precious little about this new order. Thus, before answering whether globalization is good or bad, men ought to ask and answer some basic questions. Such questions refer to the meaning of life, the importance of the family, the essence of nations, the evolution and purpose of mankind, and even others. It seems that the world has arrived at a crossroad and it may soon be confronted with a conflict of global proportions. It may be a catastrophic war in the Middle East, a global financial collapse, or a huge natural disaster. Nobody knows and it appears that we are all groping for answers. Decades ago, an older friend once wrote me that *during the next conflict every man will fight everyone else and the front line will go straight through our hearts.* It appears that we have arrived at this point. Should we sell our souls for material goods, or we should look into our hearts in search for a spiritual answer?

The process of globalization and the New World Order are affecting directly or indirectly everything and everybody from the global and national levels down to the individuals. The very identity of people is in question. As persons, we identify first and foremost with our families and with our national values. We also identify with our faith and with what "we believe" to be true. Problem is that by discarding old national values and identities without acquiring a "global consciousness," people may find themselves "culturally naked." That brings us to the "cultural pyramid." (44)

We Humans are unique creatures. We "do come" from nature, but by the time "we leave" this world we have a spiritual dimension and many of us hope to advance to a higher level of existence. Thus, in order to function harmoniously, humanity needs to understand the meaning and purpose of life. A good way to understand ourselves, as individuals, as nations, and as cultures, is to visualize a pyramid. We start at the bottom where we make a living by interfering with nature; then, as we grow up and evolve, we slowly climb up the pyramid ladder from the lower rungs of behavior and attitude, to the middle rungs of values and beliefs. Eventually, we mature and reach the spiritual top of the cultural pyramid where we start to understand the meaning of life.

For most people the meaning of life is explained by religion, by philosophy, by science, or by a combination of all of them. Together they give us our world-views, which in turn mold our beliefs and shape our values. At the bottom of the cultural pyramid our behavior reflects the interaction between us and nature, as well as among ourselves. Interacting with each other is governed by morality laws, which means pretty much the much heralded Human Rights of today. For many people, however, spiritual meaning comes from our faith, from belief in a Divine will. God must exist! In this vein, when reminded of the "irrationality" of their faith and when told that they cannot explain the very existence of God, believers point out that science cannot explain the spiritual nature of man either. And they add that *"we can explain the existence of consciousness, but we do not know why there is consciousness,"* and also *"reason cannot explain why there is reason."*(45) Therefore, why not take the leap of faith?

If the Divine does not exist, or if He is banned, every kind of behavior would be acceptable and the powerful will try to replace God. Globalization is only about what we do without explaining the higher purpose or meaning of life. Can we and should we restrict ourselves to blind materialism? Should we believe the promise of the globalists about future benefits for all? They may be able to create a world full of material goods, a sort of God-less paradise on earth, but it will be "a hell of a paradise." This is what the communists tried to do in Russia for seventy years and in East Europe for fifty years. Looking back at the Marxist-Leninist regimes under which I grew up, I am pondering about their true purpose. What did they want to do and who was behind them? It is increasingly clear to me that those regimes had three goals in mind: to uproot God and especially Christianity from the souls of the people; to weaken nations and destroy nationalism: and to frighten people so deeply as to accept any alternative. And the alternative seems to be globalization under a new world order.

As for nations, they are well-established communities of very long duration reflecting a material and objective reality, as well as a subjective and spiritual one. And the two dimensions, one visible tying us to nature and to each other and the other invisible and tying us to the Divine, are linked and must develop in harmony. And nations prosper under liberty when they have enlightened leaders, educated populations, and when they come across the right conjuncture. Such conjunctures are major events that can change history. Yet, even the best conjunctures can be annulled by corrupt leaders, by indifferent populations, and by persistent vicious circles. (46)

Is globalization a new world conjuncture or another vicious circle? Is it going to bring about a balanced development, wide-spread economic wellness, and spiritual emancipation? Or it will come with even more social polarization, concentration of wealth in the hands of a few, and spiritual emptiness? The paramount fear is that given the ruthless competition at the top between corporations, whoever will win the global race for power and wealth will have to be ruthlessly evil. God help us!

From a worldly standpoint, respected social thinkers, such as Christian Kopf and many others, consider that the biggest division of our time is *"not between Right and Left, but between Nations and the Globalist delusion."* (47) I arrived at the same conclusion long before reading his statement and that means troubles. The process of globalization is more than a deadly struggle between nations and globalists; it is a deadly spiritual confrontation between those who believe and those who hate the idea of God; actually, between good and evil. Indeed, responsible researchers have concluded that if the current trends continue and if the beliefs, values, and interests of average people are not addressed properly the world could end up in a terrible crisis. They stress that greed and myopia brought down the elites in France in 1789 and in Russia in 1917, and the leaders of those countries did not expect their own demise. (48) The difference is that in the era of globalization the catastrophe can reach global proportions. Globalization seems to represent the plan of the rich and powerful to organize a world without God. Even if their intentions are good, remember again that *the road to hell is paved with good intentions* . . . And the reader may still wait for an answer.

Please, look into your heart and find it!

* * *

PART TWO—
REGIONAL ISSUES

GLOBALIZATION, POLITICS
AND GEOPOLITICS

Globalization is chiefly about economic integration. However, economic integration is fostered by political actions and together they often end up in geopolitics. The European Union, for example, started with economic integration, but currently advances fast toward a political union. The North American Free Trade Agreement is strictly economic for now, but it will undoubtedly move toward a political integration if allowed to run its full course. On the other hand, Russia's economic moves especially toward Europe are from the start geopolitical in nature. China and Southeast Asia, however, represent a case of complex economic connections with no current plans of full integration. Yet, the economic rise of China causes geopolitical fears in East Asia. This section of the study focuses on these four important regions of the world.

I — Europe and the European Union

In many ways Europe is a blessed continent. It has an excellent location on the globe, it enjoys a healthy climate, it has a good combination of land forms and agricultural sources, and it has had a rather good start in modern history. Europe also inherited the Christian attitude toward nature and toward personal achievements, which gave it the impetus to dominate the world for some 500 years. On the negative side, Europe is open to the vast lands of Asia, and in the past it has been open for centuries to eastern invasions. The brunt of those invasions was borne by the eastern part of the continent and they are still visible these days. Economically, Europe is endowed with rather limited minerals and energy resources, which makes it dependent on foreign imports. From a political point of view, having been divided most of the time in scores of states, the history of Europe is very much a history of wars. And World War II was a catastrophe. At the end of the war, a good part of the continent was in ruins. Yet, after many rounds of negotiations, most of Europe has become a political union and an economic powerhouse. How did it all happen?

THE EUROPEAN UNION—THE MOST ADVANCED INTEGRATED BLOC IN THE WORLD

After over fifty years in the making, the European Union (EU) is a firm reality today affecting the lives of its inhabitants and making its impact felt throughout the entire world. Is the integration of Europe just an experiment or a trend to be emulated in the era of globalization? And then, how far can the European Union expand? What are the benefits and downfalls of joining the union? And what lessons can other regions of the world draw from the integration of Europe? Hypothetically, it appears that from a political point of view the EU has become a guarantor of peace and security for all its members. Economically, however, it has helped mainly the rich and powerful Western countries, while the new Eastern members have had limited benefits. Yet, other countries of the East are eager to join the union.

As of 2012, the EU has 27 member countries with a total surface area of 4.5 million square kilometers and a population of about 500 million. Within its brief history, the EU has extended almost to its natural borders, that is, from the Atlantic Ocean in the west to the Baltic Sea in the northeast and the Black Sea in the southeast of the continent. Consequently, Europe is now a powerful bloc especially from an economic point of view. Politically, however, the EU is not a union in the strict sense, at least not yet, and from an ethnic point of view its people continue to identify with their original nations. However, old animosities have considerably diminished in most areas of the continent, and the Europeans are now increasingly open to emphasizing their common heritage and mutual interests. It is indeed a huge difference when compared to the prewar situation when the Europeans almost destroyed themselves. How did the EU become what it is today?

PRELUDE TO THE EU

Unified for the first time since the Roman Empire, during the last half century Europe has known a period of peace, stability and prosperity without precedent in modern times. Two thousand years ago, the Romans unified a large part of Europe, but they did it by conquest and without any plan of unification. Since then, several leaders and powers had tried to unify and control the continent, but their attempts failed. Worth mentioning are Charlemagne in the 9th Century and Napoleon at the beginning of the 19th Century. During the 20th Century, the former Soviet Union tried to unify as much of Europe as possible under communist regimes controlled by Moscow. Germany also occupied and controlled a good part of Europe during World War II. If the German occupation was short, the Soviet control of East Europe lasted about 45 years. Both attempts were brutal and failed because they were forced from outside and were contrary to the interests of the occupied nations.

Europe 2000 AD. Source: Wikipedia

During the postwar years, Moscow forced its model on East Europe and tried to expand the Soviet empire while Western Europe started the process of integration. In time, the Western countries advanced and prospered and offered an enviable model to the countries of the East. For the Eastern nations which had lived in poverty and without personal liberty for decades, the EU had become a panacea and a paradise they dreamt of joining for years. When the time came, the reality of joining turned to be somehow sour, but it was a much better alternative than living under the Soviet system. Nevertheless, the foundation and expansion of the EU came in a democratic way and with the consent of the people. At the same time, the process was gradual allowing the Eastern governments and citizens to prepare and to adjust to the new system. However, the people were not necessarily informed about the next steps and stages of the union and about what the future would hold for them. At times, the results caught many countries by surprise. So far, however, the integration of Europe has brought more positive results than shortcomings, and the majority of the people seem to accept the new reality.

EU EVOLUTION

For centuries Europe has represented the archetype system of the "nation-states" with all their unique achievements and downfalls. As achievements, nation-states have brought about internal cohesion and a sense of community. As downfall, they caused excessive nationalism and the potential for conflicts and wars. Yet, the traditional European nation-state was a stable form of territorial organization. In general, inside the nation-state people share a common history, inhabit their own country, and feel like belonging together. Economically, nation-states offer a closed and often protected market that traditionally is able to satisfy the needs of their people. A note of caution is needed here. Nation-states are not immutable. They evolve, they change, and they may even disappear. Yet, nation-states have served and are still serving mankind rather well. Those who rush to dismiss them as old-fashioned, as well as those who consider them immutable, are wrong. The pertinent question is: Are nation-states currently withering away naturally? Or are some forces trying to bury them?

The reality is that the modern world with its global reach has made economic integration a necessity, but the process has been slow and full of internal and external controversies. And that has created problems of domestic and international adjustments. For example, until the middle of the 20th Century Europe was in the center of the world. Then, within a span of only fifty years everything changed and Europe lost its international preeminence. However, that was the period when the formerly split continent became a union. Consequently, countries, governments, businesses, and people had to adjust to a new reality.

It appears that at the beginning of the 21st Century, regional integration and globalization are here to stay. But, while integrating economically, people's mentality lags behind, being stuck in the mental frame of the nation-state. Understanding this ambiguity was very important for the framers of the EU who emphasized that the EU was a union of equal and sovereign nation-states. The reality, however, is that member countries have already lost a great deal of their sovereignty and independence. It has been a trade-off. In return for losing some of the prerogatives of national sovereignty, people have gained more security, increased freedom of movement, and new individual opportunities. Yet, many Europeans feel that they are now under two sets of bureaucracy and some of them doubt that what they got is what they expected. Along these lines some delicate questions have been raised causing reticence and frustration. Such questions deal with, for example, unchecked freedom of movement, new problems related to social assistance and health care, reallocation of economic aid, and others. Yet, the integration of Europe has continued.

Historically, the unification of Europe started with the Treaty of Paris signed on December 18, 1951, which established the European Coal and Steel Community. It was a limited cooperation agreement, but it proved pivotal. The idea was originally launched by the French sociologist Jean Monet who identified the competition for resources, especially between France and Germany, as a permanent source of friction. Konrad Adenauer, German chancellor at the time, recognized the importance of the idea and embraced it. At that time, Western Europe was still suffering the consequences of the war and was looking for new ways to ensure a better future. Italy, Netherlands, Belgium and Luxembourg adhered rather quickly to the idea. Those initial six countries signed the Treaty of Paris aimed at eliminating the root cause of war in Europe. The success of the initial treaty made them take another step forward and to conclude the Treaty of Rome. That treaty was signed on March 25, 1957, and established the European Economic Community (EEC). It was this new treaty that actually launched the process of integration. If the first steps were strictly economic, the next steps began to be political. During the same year a European Court of Justice was created and in 1968 a Custom Union was formed. It is worth noting that all the initial member countries of the EEC were also members in the North Atlantic Treaty Organization (NATO). Ever since, the two organizations have tried to expand together, but membership in one of them does not condition membership in the other.

The formation of the new community in 1957 triggered a reaction among the countries that for various reasons did not join it. Thus, in 1960 Austria, Denmark, Norway, Portugal, Sweden, Switzerland, and the United Kingdom established their own community of interests named the European Free Trade Association (EFTA). With the passage of time, however, the EFTA members realized the advantages of membership in the EEC and later most of them joined it. Indeed, from the initial and small coal and steel community, the core countries of Western Europe advanced gradually but steadily toward a political union. Then, events followed as in a chain reaction. Here are the most important landmarks. The EEC set up the European Council, the staging post of the EU, which in turn in 1978 established a European Currency Unit (ECU), the precursor of the Euro. Then, in 1985 they signed the Schengen Agreement which set up a plan to work toward a common territory without inner borders and toward a common frontier. The next step was signing the Treaty of Maastricht in February 1992. The signatory countries decided to establish a full European government, which also included a Parliament. Three years later the new currency of the European Union (Euro) was introduced and most members discarded their old money. As of 2012 only the UK and Denmark did not join the new currency, considering it an infringement on their sovereignty.

Today the EU has a new headquarters in Brussels and it has its own executive, legislative and judiciary branches. A new bureaucracy is taking over the affairs of the old continent. As a result, laws are now written by the new bureaucracy and they represent up to 80 percent of all European legislation. Furthermore, the EU is working hard to create new super-state institutions to take over the national ones, such as a common defense and police force. At the same time, the union is open to further expansion.

THE INTEGRATION OF EAST EUROPE

The disintegration of the Eastern bloc in the late 1980s and early 1990s, and the dissolution of the Soviet Union, opened the possibility of expanding the EU eastward. The East European countries were not prepared for such a huge change, but the decision to expand was taken in Brussels and other important western capitals. The new Europe wanted to be together regardless of the economic cost involved in the process. As a result, the expansion was rapid, yet gradual. To ease their integration, the new member countries were granted a period of grace before changing their laws to accord with the EU laws and before switching to the new currency.

The cooptation of Eastern Europe into the EU is an interesting case. Integration in the EU has been a long lasting objective of many eastern people, but it came with negative side effects as well. To begin with, no one has explained yet why Eastern Europe was left in Moscow's grip for almost 50 years. Was this the direct result of the Yalta agreements? Did the Yalta agreements have some secret protocols like the Soviet-German Pact of 1939? And if so, what agreements were concluded at Malta in 1989 between the United States and the Soviet Union and what are their unpublished provisions?

The sad reality is that the Eastern European countries were not offered any real choice either in 1944 when they were invaded by the Soviet troops, or after 1989 when the communist camp disintegrated. It is true that after the tragic communist experience every eastern nation wanted to join the EU, but the integration came at some unexpected cost. If the old regimes, for example, had built industries to allegedly offer workers employment, the EU integration came with ravaging deindustrialization followed by a painful host of social problems. It is also true that most of the communist-built plants were not profitable, but even many of those that were lucrative were ruined. The West insisted that the economies of the Eastern countries be privatized. To this effect, Western officials and private investors cooperated with whoever they found in charge, almost all former communist activists and secret police officers, for their mutual interests. Morality was nonexistent. Slowly, East Europe was very much de-industrialized.

Accordingly, during the decade of the 1990s, members of the former East European nomenclature privatized the state economies for their personal benefits. Worst still, the former communists became the new political elite of today's East Europe. As a former Russian human rights advocate put it recently *"the sons and daughters of our former masters became the masters of our sons and daughters."* While average eastern workers make now a few hundred dollars per month, many new "businessmen" became multi-millionaires. And in Russia, there are even billionaires (in US dollars). There is indeed a lot more individual freedom in today's East Europe, but the old communists and the new crooks have used the new freedom to their advantage. They have profited from the dominant positions inherited from the past and from the condoning attitude of the West, America included.

Modern Thinking Man by Auguste Rodin (1849-1917)

At the end of the communist regime, Romania for example, had one of the largest commercial fleets in the world. After the fall of the regime the fleet was bankrupted ship by ship and sold for next to nothing to shady foreign businessmen who bribed Romanian officials with millions of dollars. Of the one hundred ocean-going ships that Romania had in 1989, today it only has *one*. The same big ships that were supposedly too old to navigate the oceans are still sailing profitably for the new international owners. They were sold because the West insisted on the privatization of the state industries. In the steel industry the situation was even more dramatic. Romania was allowed to export to the EU only about two million metric tons of steel annually, but its annual capacity was over ten million tons. Consequently, a good part of the steel industry, including brand new installations, were dismantled and sold as scrap iron to the same EU that rejected the Romanian steel. Other industries with competitive counterparts in the West were bought by those counterparts and then bankrupted to eliminate any possible competition. The results have been widespread demoralization and the polarization of the society between the *nouveau rich* and the new poor. Nevertheless, the fear of its traditional nemesis, namely Russia, and remembering the atrocities of communism, made Romania eagerly join NATO and to celebrate its acceptance into the EU. If the communist past was disastrous and if the present is still difficult, at least now people have hopes for a better future. At long last, the Romanians, as well as the other East European nations, feel safe as part of a unified Europe. But where is Europe going?

Currently, the EU has 27 member countries. They are the six founding members: Belgium, Germany, France, Italy, Luxembourg and the Netherlands; Denmark, Ireland and the United Kingdom that joined the six initial countries in 1973; Greece which joined in 1981; Portugal and Spain that followed in 1986; and Austria, Finland and Sweden which joined the union in 1995. Then, the biggest enlargement ever occurred on 1 May 2004 when 10 Eastern countries, namely the Czech Republic, Estonia, Cyprus, Latvia, Lithuania, Hungary, Malta, Poland, Slovenia, and Slovakia joined the European Union.

Bulgaria and Romania joined the club on 1 January 2007, bringing the current membership to 27 countries.

The European Union 2007 (darker shade)

ACHIEVEMENTS AND UNWANTED SIDE EFFECTS

The most significant achievement of Europe under the EU is that for the first time in a long period the continent is safe. It no longer fears German expansions or Russian invasions. Paralleling the EU with membership in NATO has given the area a security never known in the past. From an economic point of view, however, the story is different. The annual GDP per capita in the West, for example, is several times bigger than in the East. According to Wikipedia, and as estimated by the IMF, in 2010 per capita GDP was over 45,000 dollars in France as compared to about 12,000 in Poland and 7,500 in Romania. (According to the same article, however, CIA estimated Romania's per capita GDP at 9,600 dollars). By other estimates, incomes are even smaller in the East. The economic integration of the Western countries was successful because those countries were highly and rather equally developed. The addition of the Eastern countries brought along some advantages to both sides, but it also added to the cost of developing the new areas. The integration made the EU more uneven and it deepened the internal disparities. Nevertheless, the fact that after their integration Greece and Portugal were pulled out of relative poverty and that Ireland was transformed into a successful story encouraged the newly integrated countries. They also hope that the current financial crisis in Greece is only temporary. Thus, for the time being the situation is not rosy for East Europe, but there is hope and guarded optimism.

The expansion of the union has also come with new problems for both sides. Lack of opportunities at home and income disparities have made many East Europeans leave their countries and seek employment in the West. Membership in the EU allows them freedom of circulation, but finding adequate jobs is not easy. Most of the migrants have to accept any jobs regardless of their education or skills. Consequently, they accept smaller wages than the Western workers and this in turn often deprives the latter of potential employment and negotiation capabilities. While the big corporations profit, Western employees become frustrated and Eastern migrants are caught in between.

CURRENT EU MEMBERSHIP
(ALPHABETICAL ORDER)

Country	Population (mil.)	Area (Sq. Km)	Date of Admission
Austria	8.4	83,881	1 January 1995
Belgium	10.5	30,528	25 March 1957
Bulgaria	7.6	110,910	1 January 2007
Cyprus	0.8	9,251	1 May 2004
Czech Rep.	10.4	78,866	1 May 2004
Denmark	5.5	43,094	1 January 1973
Estonia	1.3	45,226	1 May 2004
Finland	5.3	338,415	1 January 1995
France	63.8	674,843	25 March 1957
Germany	82.2	357,050	25 March 1957
Greece	11.1	131,990	1 January 1981
Hungary	10.0	93,030	1 May 2004
Ireland	4.3	70,273	1 January 1973
Italy	59.6	301,318	25 March 1957
Latvia	2.3	64,589	1 May 2004
Lithuania	3.4	65,303	1 May 2004
Luxembourg	0.5	2,586	25 March 1957
Malta	0.4	316	1 May 2004
Netherlands	16.4	41,526	25 March 1957
Poland	38.1	312,682	1 May 2004

Portugal	10.6	92,391	1 January 1986
Romania	21.5	238,391	1 January 2007
Slovakia	5.4	49,037	1 May 2004
Slovenia	2.0	20,273	1 May 2004
Spain	46.0	506,030	1 January 1986
Sweden	9.2	449,964	1 January 1995
U K	60.6	244,820	1 January 1973
Total EU	497.5	4,456,324	1957-2007

Sources: "Member States of the European Union," *Wikipedia—The Free Encyclopedia*, August 2008; *The World Almanac and Book of Facts*, New York: World Almanac Books, 2007

The human side of the integration has also come with its own negative effects. Millions of young men and women have already left East Europe to work in the West. In Romania, for example, ten percent of the country's population, that is over two million mostly young people, left for different Western countries. Many of those people have managed to send home monthly remittances that have kept their countries afloat, but the social effects at home were sometimes somber. With men gone to work in the West oftentimes separated families end up in divorce and children grow up with no supervision and with no good parental models to emulate. Furthermore, by Western standards, the countryside of East Europe is overpopulated and it has been suggested that the "surplus" people should move to the depopulated rural areas of the West. It appears that what the Soviets could not achieve through sheer brutality is being achieved now with sweetened pills.

The newly found freedom in the East also came with such social ills as prostitution, human trafficking, drugs, gambling, corruption and crime. Shady dealers on both sides of the former Iron Curtain do business now in many of these fields. Most of these social ills were imported from the West. Consequently, for many East Europeans the once admired West has lost its credibility and its former high moral ground. At the same time, while the Western companies have extended their reach to the east, East Europe has remained mainly a source of cheap labor and of new markets to be conquered. And since the East European countries do not have the financial resources to sustain themselves during the prolonged transition to Western-types of economies, they borrow heavily from the West. The result is that the international debt of East Europe is now staggering.

At the same time, while Western companies are extending their businesses to the East, the EU officials are micromanaging everything and people have no recourse against it. For example, the number of hectares to be cultivated with certain crops in each country, the way of making wine, the quantity of cheese to be exported, the packaging of goods, et cetera, must meet the standards prescribed by the new European bureaucracy. And in the future even personal behavior and family habits must be changed including, as an example, the traditional butchering of animals at home by farmers. As a result, the past is fast disappearing in East Europe while the future is not there yet. A whole way of life will soon be gone . . . and all with good intentions! Among the real beneficiaries are the big international corporations that take advantage of the situation. Yet, joining the EU remains the goal of several more European countries.

The evolution of the EU has not been without problems in the West either, and Great Britain is a good case in point. In his book *Britain Held Hostage*, Lindsay Jenkins claims that British sovereignty was signed away to Brussels and that the country is losing its independence. Furthermore, the author laments that the public was deceived to join the EU through projects and presentations that were unintelligible for most people. According to the author, England has already lost its fishing industry and some lucrative agricultural activities. Also, several Danish politicians have claimed that Denmark's accession to the EU has been unconstitutional because it by-passed the sovereignty of its parliament. No wonder that the two countries have so far rejected the Euro currency.

Lindsay Jenkins also fears that the EU is advancing toward a socialist super-state that could become a dictatorship. In this regard, the well-known Soviet dissident Vladimir Bukovski is even blunter. He makes a parallel between the organization and administration of the former Soviet Union and the European Union and gives the people an alarming signal. Interestingly, even the last Soviet leader, Mikhail Gorbachev, expressed his fear about the future of Europe. Some people fear indeed that the EU is a poisonous pill and are afraid for the future of the continent. The truth is that Western Europe is chiefly guided and manipulated by leftists, some of them actually closet Marxists, who want to implement a socialist plan of development. Little wonder the former communists of East Europe are welcome with open arms by their EU comrades. Is this trend also pursued with good intentions? Many people doubt it!

FURTHER ENLARGEMENT
AND PERSPECTIVES

Currently, the majority of the European countries are already EU members. Some of the most prosperous countries, however, notably Switzerland and Lichtenstein, Norway and Iceland, have opted against joining the union. On the other hand, several small Balkan countries do not qualify yet for membership, but they are encroached by the EU and will most likely be integrated in the future. In this regard, the union has stressed that in order to become a member a country must meet the criteria set by the Copenhagen Council of June 1993. They are defined as: the stability of institutions guaranteeing democracy; the rule of law; human rights and protection of minorities; a functioning market economy; the capacity to cope with competitive pressure and market forces within the EU; and the ability to take on the obligations of membership including adherence to the aims of political, economic and monetary union. In this light Croatia, Macedonia and Turkey are considered strong candidates. In addition, Albania, Bosnia, Serbia, Montenegro, as well as Kosovo, are considered potential candidates. Negotiations have also been initiated with Moldova. Adding these small countries to the EU will give Europe increased geopolitical stability, but it will also exacerbate its economic woes.

Of the remaining countries, Ukraine aspires to integrate itself into the EU, but Moscow is strongly opposed on geopolitical and economic grounds. On the other hand, Turkey is very vocal in its desire to join, but in a tacit way Europe appears to be against it for cultural reasons. The republic of Belarus, the last European country left out of any consideration, has so far opted for the Russian sphere. Further to the southeast in the Caucasus Mountains, where Europe meets and mixes with Asia, Armenia has opted for the Russian sphere, Azerbaijan is inclining toward the West, and Georgia would very much like to join both NATO and the EU. However, as the world has already seen, Russia put its foot down and in August 2008 launched a full scale attack against Georgia and dismembered it. Russia, the largest country in the world straddling two continents and endowed with huge natural resources, is not interested in joining any super-state that will bring directives from outside. Although it has accepted to be a member of the Council of Europe, Russia has kept its own agenda.

In the meantime, the EU is searching for its own constitution and for a new sense of identity. Unfortunately, the big Western European leaders and the leftists behind them refuse to acknowledge the undeniable Christian heritage of the continent. What could the future be if the EU denies its own culture and religion? Can the much heralded human rights replace religion in general and Christianity in particular? Or, in the name of freedom, Europe will become a godless place? The truth is that what unifies the Europeans is exactly their culture and the most important part of it is the Christian religion. What spiritual model will the EU offer to the rest of the world if it denies its own past?

And there is one more problem. Europe has been fragmented for most if its history. In a way, this fragmentation did not allow any country total domination over the continent and saved European democracy. By contrast, Russia and China for example, have been strongly centralized for most of their histories, but their centralization fed despotism and ended up in dictatorships. There were dictatorships in Europe, too, but at any time there were also free and democratic countries. When the entire continent will be unified under one government the prospect of dictatorship could become real.

Integration, globalization, cultural plurality, and human fraternity are all beautiful concepts, but are the people of the world ready for these ideals? If national governments lose their sovereign rights who will monitor in the future those who control the process of globalization? It is said that if one wants to boil a live lobster, one must put it in cold water and heat it up slowly. The lobster will not feel the gradual change in temperature and will get boiled without even noticing its own death. Some Europeans already fear for the future of their countries and of the continent. Yet, the EU is already the model for integration for other regional blocs, including for North America.

II—The United States and NAFTA

Protected by two oceans and endowed with rich resources, the United States of America has enjoyed security, freedom, and prosperity for most of its existence. Within about one hundred years from its independence, the young United States became a quasi-continental country and a dominant world power. However, in the process of expansion Washington alienated some of its hemispheric neighbors who still remember with wariness the dominant Anglo-Saxon USA. Yet, Washington has tried hard in recent decades to promote democracy in Latin America and to integrate them into an economic cooperation bloc. The most important initiative in this regard is the North American Free Trade Agreement (NAFTA). This agreement aims at bringing together the economies of the United States, Canada, and Mexico. In this regard, North America seems to be trying to emulate the European Union. Is this feasible or desirable as some scholars propose? Will the average "American" citizen benefit from a union with Mexico and Canada?

THE NORTH AMERICAN COMMUNITY AND THE EUROPEAN MODEL

The integration of North America should hypothetically bring about more goods for everybody, but it may also hurt US employment and it would lead to an erosion of national sovereignty. That does not exclude the idea of deepening the cooperation between the United States, Canada and Mexico. On the contrary, the three countries should do everything to extend their trade and cooperation and to increase the efforts aiming at understanding each other ever better. As it has been postulated, the exchange of goods, people and ideas is the best way to achieve integration. Other than that, however, global human brotherhood is a long way off and is questionable if it will ever be achieved. World reality is very much different. We continue to encounter conflicting cultural, political and economic interests. And the current global financial and economic problems are not helping either.

As it has already been discussed in the previous chapter, the idea of integrating different parts of the world, mainly for the interest of the integrator, is as old as mankind. Modern integration through mutual agreements and for the common good of all is rather recent and the EU is the model to pursue. But could it be duplicated by the rest of the world and especially by North America? It should be recalled that the EU was born out of necessity and it was initially a Western organization of equally developed countries with rather similar cultures. At the time, Europe was exhausted after two devastating wars and was under the threat of communism and the Soviet Union. Yet, it took 50 years of hard and continuous negotiations to get to the current status. And it is not yet sure if the EU will be equally successful in integrating Eastern Europe. Can North America follow the same path?

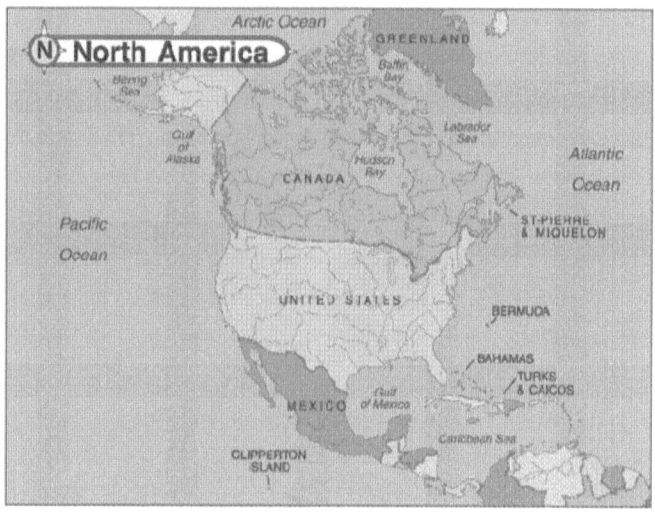

The United States, Canada and Mexico. Source: Wikipedia

Unlike Western Europe, the three North American countries have different cultural and geopolitical experiences, different aspirations, different economic and population dynamics, and, more importantly, they are not threatened by anybody. In addition, while economically and geopolitically Western Europe has always been multipolar, North America has always been strongly unipolar with the United States dominating the continent. From this point of view, North America does not need a political union to allay the fear of wars as Europe did. Neither Mexico nor Canada is capable or willing to challenge the United States. On the contrary, Canada needs the United States to better defend its space and Mexico needs it for economic reasons.

From a cultural point of view, most Canadians are almost indistinguishable from "Americans" and in addition ten percent of all of them live currently in the United States. Mexicans, however, are rather different. Most of them are racially mixed and have different values, mentalities and expectations. Most Mexicans do share a European language and religion and are rather open to the Anglo-Saxon world of the north, but do not seem to be willing to change their traditional culture and assimilate to a new one. At the same time, from an economic point of view, the differences between the United States and Canada on one hand and Mexico on the other are huge. The result is that an integration of the three countries will be more difficult than the integration of Europe.

The historical experiences of Mexico and Canada are also different and make them approach the United States with apprehension. The Americans, for example, are proud of the 1776 revolution and the unique Constitution of the United States. However, while the Americans revolted against England, the English-speaking Canadians remained loyal to the mother country which they respect to this day. Had the United States taken Canada during the 19th Century, in time the Canadians would have probably settled peacefully as American citizens. The Canadians, however, remained close to England and in time they acquired a different mentality and attitude toward life as well as a different political system. Now they see the "American" society as arrogant and invasive, as prone to violence, and as threatening to their life-style. The reality is that as long as the United States exists, the Canadians will probably have a complex and will feel relegated to the status of a sub-nation.

Consequently, it is doubtful that the Canadians would accept a political union with the United States. Contrary to what some scholars may claim, for now free trade and economic cooperation appears to be just enough for Canada.

As for Mexico, its historical experience with the United States is even less conducive to a future union. While marching toward the Pacific, the young United States came across Spanish-speaking lands peopled by Mexicans. In time, a huge area of Mexico was annexed by the United States through wars or trough various treaties. The Mexicans did not forget the annexations of their land, and many of them still view with ambiguity the southwestern part of the United States where many of them continue to live. Granted, the Mexican-Americans prefer to be part of the United States, but most of them continue to identify as Mexicans. And modern Mexico at large did not forget its historical experience either. An old adage even states that the problem of Mexico is that *it is too far from God and too close to the United States*. Actually, many Mexicans perceive the United States as acting superior, arrogant, and patronizing. Nonetheless, given the opportunity, millions of Mexicans would like to come to the United States either to work temporarily or to settle for good. Thus, unlike the Canadians, who are worried about maintaining their identity and life-style and about controlling their natural resources, most Mexicans would greet an opening of the US border. In this regard, they hope that the NAFTA treaty is just a beginning. No wonder the Mexican leaders have advocated amnesty for the Mexicans who live illegally in the United States and an opening of the US-Mexican border.

The attitude toward a continental integration and the perception of NAFTA in the United States is rather different. In reality, most Americans do not know much about the treaty or about proposals for deeper integration. Yet, after the ratification of the treaty many of them began to fear an inflow of Mexicans pouring over the border and bringing with them a host of problems. Nonetheless, since its inception the treaty has scored some positive achievements, but it also has triggered negative consequences, predicted and feared by those who oppose it.

NAFTA: HISTORY AND ACHIEVEMENTS

The North American Free Trade Agreement went into effect in January 1994 after several years of negotiations. Its purpose was to reduce and to gradually eliminate any barriers to trade and investments among the United States, Mexico and Canada. For now, that means very much American capital, Canadian resources, and Mexican labor. The possibility was left open to enlarge the organization by integrating other countries of the Americas as well. Since its inception NAFTA has brought about a number of advantages and disadvantages to the people of the three countries. However, south of the border Mexican expectations of free migration to the United States have not been fulfilled, and north of the border many Americans still do not see the advantages of merging the markets. As for its part, Canada seems to remain aloof and to follow, albeit reluctantly, the US lead. In addition, there are a number of projects that make some people worry.

US, CANADA AND MEXICO—BASIC DATA

Country	Square Miles	Population in Millions	Population under 15	Per capita GDP
USA	3,719,000	300	20.6 %	$ 46,000
Canada	3,855,000	33	17.9 %	$ 39,000
Mexico	762,000	103	31.1 %	$ 13,000
Total	8,336,000	436		

Source: The World Almanac, New York: 2008, Google Research, 2009

The projected North American Superhighway, for example, is considered by many small businessmen as a Trojan horse and a danger to traditional American ways. It is a system of huge highways and pipes connecting the Mexican seaports with the interior of the United States. Such links would bypass the American harbors on the West Coast, where unionized workers earn good salaries, and would bring foreign goods carried by Mexican trucks directly into the middle of the continent. From there the goods would be redistributed throughout the United States and further north to Canada. It is probably expected that in a future fully globalized world, North America will be the center of the world, the United States will be the continent's epicenter, and this highway will become the aorta of the new world. According to existing plans, this project would be built by private/public partnerships and would charge big tolls for the people using it. However, since trucks would no longer be checked at the ports of entry, the danger of illicit traffic would increase, and the entire system would further erode American sovereignty. The project is already under way.

NAFTA Projected Highways

The North American integration also poses demographic, cultural, and political problems for the United States. With the Mexican population under 15 years of age at 31 percent and with a much higher demographic increase, Mexico already has an excess of people. Consequently, with limited employment opportunities at home, many young Mexicans will try to come legally or illegally to the United States. It has been already estimated that up to 70 million Mexicans would be willing to come to the United States. According to other sources, only 15 million are determined to come. Either way, such a move would place undue stress on the American economy and life-style and would be detrimental to Mexico as well. Along with them, the Mexican immigrants would bring problems of health care, unemployment benefits, schooling, social security, drugs, gangs and most likely, increased violence. Will the United States be willing to put up with such consequences?

CULTURAL AND POLITICAL ISSUES FOR THE US

Generally, most Mexican immigrants have adapted well to life in the United States, but the past trends reveal that they do not assimilate. The late Harvard scholar Samuel Huntington also pointed toward the same conclusion. Even without more Mexican immigration the Latin American population in the United States is going to increase fast in the future. According to a recent study by the *Pew Research Center*, the proportion of the US Latin population is going to grow from the current 17 percent to over 30 percent by the year 2060. The result may be that southwest United States would revert to its previous Hispanic culture and in time the rest of the country will have to learn Spanish. Actually, recent projections foresee that before the middle of the century the white population of the United States will shrink to less than fifty percent. And within this diminishing share the Anglo-Saxons will become a minority. As a consequence, the traditional American life-style will be changed and traditional America may cease to exist. Multiculturalism is a little understood concept. From a political point of view, once a new economy is in place and the life-style is changed, politics will follow suit and democracy may become a thing of the past. Yet, none of these potential consequences seem to bother those who plan to take advantage of the future changes. But, would such changes be beneficial to average Americans?

Another important issue of a future integration is the impact on the sovereignty of the United States. Sovereignty means making your own decisions, both domestically and internationally, and applying them for the benefit of your citizens. This requires a capable, responsible, and accountable government. What will happen when decisions affecting the American citizens will be made by some strange NAFTA bureaucrats? What will happen when some omnipotent international corporations will become more powerful than the government? It is a fact that half of the biggest transnational corporations are richer than half of the independent countries of the world. If Washington is unable to control the big international corporations now, they could control Washington in the future, and the average American citizen would bear the consequences. There are already numerous attacks on national sovereignty everywhere. And there is already an undeclared war between American patriots and internationalists.

The truth is that ethno-centrism and self-interest are the main motivators of all nations, and nation-states exist to take care of all their citizens. In a multinational world dominated by transnational corporations and faceless bureaucrats, the only motivator will be profit and the beneficiaries will be the corporations themselves. The notion of "citizen" may very well disappear or will be replaced by an empty concept of global citizenship. It should be recalled that the sole purpose of the strong and powerful is to maximize profit, power and control. In antiquity, the slaves had no freedom and were given enough just to stay alive. During the Middle Ages, the serfs had limited freedom to move around and were given enough to maintain their households. Democratic capitalism was the first socio-political system that guaranteed individual freedom and tried to assure a decent standard of living for all citizens. If national governments lose their prerogatives, who is going to care for their countries' citizens?

The globalization of the world, and in this particular case the internationalization of North America, is being done allegedly for economic integration and for mutual benefits. But, is economic integration an end by itself or only just a mean to reach an end? Then, what is the end? Reading the current tea leaves, when the world will become a global market dominated by financial institutions and multinational companies, most people will be bound with invisible chains. They will be perpetually indebted to financial institutions whose purpose will be to keep them forever indebted. And all that *with good intentions!* Is NAFTA luring the United States on this path?

III — Russia between Old Geopolitics and New Economic Realities

Since the dismemberment of the Soviet Union, Moscow has had an uneasy relationship with both Western Europe and the United States. Most Russians wanted to rid themselves of communism, but they did not expect to lose their empire. Consequently, the Russians felt thoroughly frustrated by the events and had a hard time adjusting to the post-Soviet realities. Nevertheless, the era of globalization has tied Russia to the European Union. Simply, from an economic point of view, Moscow needs European technology and Europe needs Russian resources. Geopolitically, the relationship is more complicated because Moscow continues to perceive the West as a potential threat. At the same time, Russia is trying hard to control or at least to influence East Europe. This situation is further compounded by the American presence, geopolitically and economically, from the Baltic Sea to the Black and Caspian Seas. The huge energy resources of the Caspian basin, located at the periphery of Moscow's influence, only worsen the relationship. In this vein, from a Russian geopolitical and eco-political point of view, the key to its relations with the West is maintaining full control over the Ukraine and strong influence over the Caucasus region.

Russia and Ukraine—an Uneasy Relationship

Russia has a strong historical and cultural identity, but a vague geographic identity that is reflected in its never ending expansionism. Moscow views Belarus and Ukraine, for example, as special parts of Russia. Further west and south, from the Baltic republics to Moldova and from the Black Sea to the Caspian basin, the area is seen as a Russian sphere of influence. To the west, Europe and NATO under US leadership cannot be trusted. Thus, in order to promote its interests, Moscow must keep an eye out from the Baltic Sea to the Black and Caspian Seas. Had Russia given up its territorial ambitions, it would have relinquished any old claims and would have established friendly relations with all the countries that have replaced the Soviet Union. But it is obvious that Russia did not renounce its goals. *Intermarium*, a very recent and an excellent book by Marek Jan Chodakiewicz, offers a good historical background and recent analysis for understanding the old Muscovy and the new Russia.

In the new Eastern European geopolitical configuration, Moscow sees Moldova as a stepping stone toward the Balkans and as a safe outpost behind Ukraine. Yet, Ukraine is the real Gordian knot and the key to Russia's geopolitical interests in Europe. In fact, it is hardly possible for Russia to see itself as a superpower without Ukraine. Will Moscow forgo in the foreseeable future its claim over this East European country? For now, the answer is No!

Post Soviet Russia. Source: Wikipedia

Ukraine is the largest country in Europe, but it has the misfortune to exist in the shadow of Russia, a colossus that in the past had embraced to death all its neighbors. The two eastern Slavic nations are related from an ethnic and cultural point of view and for centuries they have evolved in close association. These facts make a complete separation of the two very difficult. With the passage of time, numerous Russians have settled in Ukraine, while countless Ukrainians have settled in Russia. There are also millions of mixed marriages and numerous Ukrainians have adopted Russian as their native tongue. For its part, Moscow has tried hard to minimize any differences between Russians and Ukrainians. The reality, however, is that throughout most of their history, the Russians looked down on the Ukrainians, mistreated them and neglected their aspirations. Consequently, when the Soviet Union broke apart in 1991, the

163

majority of Ukrainians rejected any new close association with Moscow. But Ukraine is politically unstable, its population is ethnically mixed, and its territory was artificially assembled by Moscow.

Historically, much of today's Ukraine descends from the "Kievan Rus," a city-state founded by Vikings that flourished one thousand years ago. In time, the state fell into internal conflicts and was successively subdued by the Tatars, by the Russians, and by the Poles. As a result of those foreign invasions, to this day modern Ukraine reveals various influences. The Tatars, who settled chiefly in the south of the country and particularly in Crimea, are Muslims of Asian origin. They were later strengthened by the Ottoman Turks who dominated the Black Sea and the southern area of Ukraine for centuries. Eastern Ukraine, located near Russia, became highly russified, a process facilitated by the Christian Orthodox religion shared by most Russians and Ukrainians. Western Ukraine, formerly under the Poles and part of it later under the Austrians, became predominantly Catholic and was well westernized. Of all the foreign occupiers, the Tatars and the Turks were indirectly the most consequential for Ukraine. Trying to defend themselves against the Turks, in 1654 the Ukrainians appealed to Moscow for help and united their land with Russia. In practical terms, that led to the annexation of their country by Moscow.

The twentieth century was very turbulent for the Ukrainians. As junior partners to Russia, the only Ukrainians who could prosper under the Tsars were those who served Moscow's interests and who assimilated with the Russians. Small wonder that after the Bolshevik Revolution Ukraine seized the opportunity and in 1918 proclaimed its short-lived independence. Four years later it was occupied by the Red Army and transformed into a Soviet republic. The event was followed by seventy years of suffering. Most Ukrainians, who were generally peasants, opposed the Soviet regime and particularly the collectivization of their land. As a consequence, the communists under Stalin engineered a murderous famine that claimed the lives of millions. That horror was so vivid among the Ukrainians that when Germany invaded the Soviet Union in 1941 many of them sided with the new occupiers. Furthermore, since many communists who persecuted the people under Stalin were Jews, when the Germans came, many Ukrainians resorted to revenge against them. All that led to new Soviet repressions in the late 1940's when more millions were starved. After Stalin's death, the situation returned to a modicum of normalcy, but any manifestation of nationalism was harshly suppressed. When finally the USSR imploded, Ukraine was among the first to proclaim its independence. Ever since, relations between Kiev (Kyiv in Ukrainian) and Moscow have been difficult, revealing a deep mutual mistrust. Nevertheless, Russia under Boris Yeltsin recognized the separation of Ukraine and Western Europe greeted the newly independent country.

Today's Ukraine

Ukraine is one of the most populous and most endowed European countries. By size alone, 233,000 square miles, it is actually the largest country in Europe, but it is still dwarfed by the enormous size of neighboring Russia. Yet, Ukraine is a rich and important country in its own right. Ukraine used to be the bread basket of Europe and under the Soviet years it did feed a large part of the population of the USSR. Although some of its soil fertility has been depleted by years of abuse, with 58 percent of its land as arable, Ukraine remains one of Europe's richest agricultural countries. Ukraine is also endowed with other important natural resources such as coal, iron ore, salt, sulfur, as well as oil and natural gas. Based on these resources and on its proximity to Russia, the former Soviet regime built a strong industry in Ukraine that included metallurgy, heavy industry, machine building, military equipment, aircraft industry, chemicals and others. However, a good part of these big industrial complexes were built in the east, where the ethnic Russians are predominant and Moscow is not about to relinquish control over them.

LARGEST EUROPEAN COUNTRIES

Country	Sq. Miles	Pop. Millions	Arable Land	Per capita GDP/ 2011
Ukraine	233,000	46,9	58 %	$ 6,000
France	212,209	60,6	33 %	$ 44,000
Germany	137,847	82,4	33 %	$ 44,000
U. K.	94,526	60,4	26 %	$ 39,000

Source: The World Almanac and Book of Facts 2006, N. Y., 2007; Wikipedia, 2012

Despite its natural resources, Ukraine's economy is not considered developed by Western standards. Its per capita GDP, for example, is considerably lower than even in Russia, but lower standards of living would not make the Ukrainians want to rejoin Russia. On the contrary, after its newly acquired independence Kiev wanted to distance itself politically as much as possible from its former master. At the same time, many Ukrainian leaders expressed their desire to join Europe and NATO, confronting Moscow with big geopolitical issues. In fact, Ukraine's attitude was decisive in sealing the destiny of the former Soviet Union. In his book, *Yeltsin: a Revolutionary Life*, Leon Aron devoted several pages to how hard Boris Yeltsin had to negotiate a new relationship between Moscow and Kiev. Actually, neither Mikhail Gorbachev nor Boris Yeltsin wanted or expected the dissolution of the Soviet Union. The dismemberment came as a shock to Moscow and to average Russians. Sadly, after 70 years of brainwashing, many Russians deluded themselves into believing that the non-Russian ethnic groups of the USSR loved them. They were in for a big surprise!

In order to avoid a total disintegration of the country, Gorbachev and Yeltsin proposed to replace the USSR with a union of sovereign states. Ukraine, however, rejected any further subordination and insisted on a simple "community of equal and independent republics" whose primary objective was to be economic. But even the road toward such a limited community was very bumpy. In the end, Ukraine chose to go its own way, but contentious problems with Moscow arose from the start. Among those thorny problems were the question of the Russian minority left in the Ukraine, the sovereignty of Crimea, the nuclear arsenal left behind by the Red Army, and the ownership of the former Soviet Black Sea Fleet.

From a political point of view, during the first years after the Soviet collapse, Ukraine was led by former Communist bosses Leonid Kravchuck and Leonid Kuchma, who in many ways acted in concert with Moscow. In December 2004, however, Viktor Yushchenko, a Western-leaning leader, was elected president. Suddenly Ukraine appeared to be on its way to real independence and the new leadership acted immediately to prove it. Among others, as reported by *Stratfor.com* on August 13, 2008, the new leadership mandated *"that all Russian naval and air forces traversing Ukrainian territory . . . give their Ukrainian counterparts a 72-hour notice on movement, destination, cargo and munitions details."* The Russian Foreign Ministry immediately called the decision a serious anti-Russian move. Moscow would not accept to lose control over Kiev and was determined to exploit any weaknesses of its former subject.

ETHNIC AND CULTURAL PROBLEMS

The most difficult obstacles for the Russians to accept Ukraine's independence are probably historical and psychological. In this vein, Aron argues that Ukraine occupies a unique place in Russia's memory and national consciousness. Accordingly, the current generation of Russians cannot reconcile themselves with the loss of their former domains and Ukraine is the key to their European reaches. It appears that Moscow might even be willing to sign some accords with the European Union and possibly join NATO if it could hold on to its former domains. But to let Ukraine join NATO and the EU separately is inconceivable for Moscow.

From an ethnic standpoint, almost one third of Ukraine's population is non-Ukrainian. About 20 percent of them are Russian and at least another 10 percent speak Russian as their mother tongue. Other important minorities are Tatars, Romanians and Poles, who also prefer Russian as a means of cross-national communication. Linguistically, the Ukrainian language is now official and mandatory, but Russian remains widespread. In addition, many Russians and Russian speakers are concentrated in eastern Ukraine and in Crimea, where they outnumber the ethnic Ukrainians. From a religious point of view, like the Russians, most Ukrainians are Orthodox Christians, but their church is almost equally split between those who belong to the Russian Patriarchate of Moscow and those who belong to the national Ukrainian Patriarchate, which is not even recognized by Moscow. The relationship between these two churches is uneasy to say the least.

GEOPOLITICAL PROBLEMS

Russia and Ukraine are split by a number of geopolitical issues and the status of Crimea is a bitter bone of contention between them. During the early Middle Ages, this peninsula was inhabited by Slavic people in the north and by Greeks and Italians living in city-states by the Black Sea in the south. Then, during the 13th and 14th centuries the peninsula was conquered by the invading Tatars who later allied themselves with the Ottoman Turks. The Turks kept Crimea from 1478 until 1774, when it was occupied by Russia. Subsequently, from 1774 until 1954 Crimea was part of tsarist and later Soviet Russia. During those centuries the proportion of Tatar inhabitants diminished, while the number of Russians and Ukrainians increased. In 1954, on the anniversary of 300 years of the Russian-Ukrainian "union," former premier Nikita Khrushchev gave Crimea to Ukraine probably as a gesture of good will. At the time, an independent Ukraine was beyond imagination. Crimea is now an autonomous republic of Ukraine with its own constitution and parliament. According to *Wikipedia*, the peninsula has an area of 10,100 square miles and a population of about two million. Of these inhabitants 58 percent are ethnic Russians, 24 percent are Ukrainians and 12 percent are Tatars, and inter-ethnic relations are not the best.

Another friction between Moscow and Kiev is posed by the former Soviet Black Sea Navy stationed in Sevastopol, the main harbor of Crimea. For years following the Soviet collapse, this navy remained a subject of dispute, and after difficult negotiations the two sides signed an agreement granting Russia most of the navy and allowing it temporary lease of the harbor. The initial agreement was due to expire in 2017, but it was extended after Moscow agreed to discount by 30 percent the price of energy delivered to Ukraine. Still, the agreement is temporary.

Today's Ukraine. Source: Wikipedia

If eastern Ukraine and Crimea are highly influenced by Russia and would side with Moscow in a possible Russo-Ukrainian conflict, western Ukraine is a different story. By historical standards, western Ukraine is a relatively recent addition to the country with lands annexed, some of them very recently, from Poland, Slovakia and Romania. In the past, this area belonged to Poland or Austria and some of its inhabitants became Catholics and acquired a Western education. To this day, these people feel like they belong to Europe rather than to Russia. In fact, they helped the modern Ukrainian renaissance and after the fall of communism have insisted on strong links

171

to Western Europe. It was also in this part of Ukraine that president Yushchenko found his largest number of supporters. However, the difference between east and west Ukraine made the noted American scholar Samuel P. Huntington write in his book, *The Clash of Civilizations,* that Ukraine is a cleft country with two different cultures. Indeed, Ukraine is roughly split along the Dnepr River with the eastern part of the country being pro-Russian and the western part being pro-European. Accordingly, it is said that in case of a conflict, Ukraine could split along cultural and linguistic lines. And if necessary, Moscow would be eager to provoke such a split.

For the time being, the best Ukrainian policy to keep the country together is to preserve the status quo and to continue to act as a bridge between Russia and Europe. But as Huntington noted, a bridge is not a strong and desirable position and it can eventually break. That reality makes the Ukrainians face a difficult dilemma. Should it be Russia or should it be the West? The dilemma was at least temporarily solved in 2009 when the former Prime Minister Viktor Yanukovich, an avowed pro-Russian politician, was elected president. The problem, however, remains, and the Russo-Ukrainian conflict is still open. One way to close this conflict would be for Russia to join NATO and the European Union. Is this possible?

Moscow's Challenge to NATO from the Baltic to the Black Sea

Membership in NATO and the European Union presupposes recognition of the territorial integrity of all neighbors, acceptance of European laws, and submission to the Brussels authorities. However, the Russia of the last 500 years that the world has known would no longer be itself if it submitted to a center other than Moscow. If it adopted the socio-political arrangements and behavior of the West, Russia could even disintegrate. For the current generation of Russians, Russia must keep to itself and must be wary of the Chinese multitude to the east and of the European influences to the west. Yet, in this era of interdependence and globalization, Moscow can no longer develop in isolation and for this reason its attitude is ambiguous. Russia envies Europe's and America's level of development and prosperity and would like to enjoy the fruits of their status, but without changing its own socio-political system. While trying to emulate some aspects of Western culture and technology, Russia has established special economic bridges with the larger European countries, such as Germany and France. However, Moscow continues to oppose NATO's eastern expansion and to fear America's global domination. And there is nothing more that Moscow would like to see than the decoupling of Western Europe from Washington. In fact, a resurgent Russia is bent on revenge and the United States is its most hated enemy.

In order to strengthen its position and to better oppose America and NATO, Moscow has put its foot down in Belarus and Ukraine and has created a three-legged geopolitical stand in Europe. The three legs are: 1) The Kaliningrad enclave to the Baltic Sea, 2) The Trans-Dniester "republic" in southeast Europe, and 3) Abkhazia by the Black Sea in the Caucasus.

Kaliningrad. This Baltic area, formerly part of East Prussia of Germany, is a militarized enclave located between

Poland and Lithuania and without a contiguous border with Russia. Yet, Kaliningrad has been part of the Russian Federation ever since the end of World War II. Also, since the war, Russia has maintained important military installations in the area, obviously directing them against NATO's northern flank. According to the article "Kaliningrad Oblast-Military," one of many articles on this subject available in *Wikipedia*, after the fall of the Soviet Union, the *"Oblast was one of the most militarized areas of the Russian Federation, and the density of military installations there was the highest in Europe."* Actually, Russia has continued to keep ground troops in this enclave, as well as naval and air force personnel. The *Washington Times*, of January 3, 2001, cited anonymous intelligence reports and claimed that for the first time since the Cold War ended Russia had transferred tactical nuclear weapons into a military base in Kaliningrad.

In order to maintain a regional balance of power in northern Europe, the American administration under President George W. Bush decided to deploy a new anti-missile defense system in Poland and the Czech Republic. To counteract the US plans, in November 2008 Russian President Medvedev declared that Moscow would deploy modern "Iskander" missiles in the area. However, on January 2009 a Russian official announced that the deployment of missiles in Kaliningrad would be reconsidered following the election of President Barack Obama. Then, in July 2009 Obama went to Moscow and discussed with President Medvedev and Prime Minister Putin a series of delicate international issues. As reported by the Romanian language paper *Ziua* on July 8, 2009, the Russian prime minister stressed that Ukraine and Georgia *"are very important to Russia."* In turn, President Obama promised that he would "*keep this in mind*." On the same day, *Pravda* wrote that Obama concluded his visit with conciliatory words toward Russia's leadership and with only mild challenges toward its behavior. By pursuing a policy of accommodation, the Obama administration caved in to the Kremlin's demands and renounced the already agreed-upon missile defense plan. Eastern Europe reacted with disbelief and had a hard time accepting the new American attitude. Moscow won just by threatening to upgrade its weapon system, and in the process Kaliningrad remained a strong Russian military outpost on the Baltic Sea.

The Trans-Dniester region (*Transnistria* in Romanian). The second leg of Russia's stand against NATO is the self-proclaimed Trans-Dniester republic. This is a small area that split from Moldova in 1989 even before Moldova declared its independence. The Republic of Moldova itself is mostly the former Romanian province of Bessarabia annexed by the Soviet Union in 1940 following the Ribbentrop-Molotov Pact. The Soviet annexation was followed by heinous crimes against the local population perpetrated by KGB troops and local communists. In 1991 the Parliament of Moldova denounced the infamous pact and this author was invited to speak in the parliament. Yet, Moldova is not much more independent now that it was under the Soviet regime.

As a native Romanian, I have recommended and pursued the reunification of Moldova with Romania. As a researcher, however, I have been shocked by the stubborness and diabolism with which Moscow clings to this small corner of the world. Every conceivable methods, from open warfare to secret police diversions and economic blackmail, have been used by Moscow and its local agents to keep Moldova under Russia.

Nicholas Dima speaking in the Moldovan Parliament, Chisinau 1991

Few people still remember, for example, the 1992 war between the Moldovan forces and the Trans-Dniester paramilitary forces. With Russian financial and military help, the Trans-Dniester region has kept its de facto independence and has become a hub of arms trafficking and other illegal activities.

On December 7, 2003, The *Washington Post* wrote that this enclave was being led by mafia-style leaders and remained an extremely dangerous place for black marketeering. The paper also noted that the area still had remnants of the Russian 14th Army with huge quantities of shells, mines, rockets, dirty warheads and other weapons ready to be sold to whoever had the cash to buy them. The situation has not changed over the last years and the area continues to represent an unending source of friction in southeast Europe. Actually, since Romania agreed to have elements of the American anti-missile shield placed on its territory, Moscow announced that it might recognize the Trans-Dniester independence and it could place "Iskander" rockets in the area. The Kaliningrad game was repeated.

Moldova and its Trans-Dester region

177

In fact, Moscow is using this region not only against Moldova, but also against Ukraine, should this country try to pursue a vigorous pro-Western policy, and against Romania and the south-eastern flank of NATO. While it is taken for granted that Kaliningrad is a Russian territory, and since Moldova has been very much forgotten, Georgia and its territorial problems are still fresh in the memory of the West. And here is the third leg of Moscow's geopolitical stand in Europe.

Abkhazia by the Black Sea. After the dissolution of the Soviet Union, to secure its position in the geopolitically important Caucasian region, Moscow instigated several local minorities to act as proxies for its own interests. The Nagorno-Karabakh region of Azerbaijan, for example, inhabited mainly by Armenians, waged a war against Baku and linked itself to Armenia. The area is now controlled by Armenia, which itself is the only Russian ally in the region. Then, when Georgia became independent and expressed its intention to join NATO, Moscow helped Abkhazia and South Ossetia to break away from Tbilisi and declare their separate independence.

Of these two Georgian areas, Abkhazia is more important geopolitically for Russia because of its location by the Black Sea close to Turkey, an American ally and an important NATO member. Instigated by Moscow and helped militarily by Russian troops, the two areas triggered bitter wars against the Georgian forces. America and the West protested the Russian military interventions, but to no avail. To this day Abkhazia and South Ossetia remain in Russian hands. Vladimir Putin, prime minister at the time and now again president of Russia, even referred to the "artificial borders" of South and North Ossetia and alluded to their possible annexation to the Russian Federation.

The Georgian regions of Abkhazia and South Ossetia

Abkhazia represents the third leg of Russia's geopolitical strategy against NATO. Given the overall importance of the Caucasus region, its proximity to the Caspian basin and the oil-rich Central Asia, and also its proximity to Israel and the troubled Middle East, the situation of Georgia deserves special attention.

The "resetting" of America's relations with Moscow has been very much a one-way street favoring Russia. Since the resetting, the United States stopped pressuring Moscow to withdraw from the Trans-Dniester area and ignored the

179

dismemberment of Georgia after the Russian aggression of 2008. Consequently, now Moscow is pursuing its traditional geopolitical and economic interests in the area. As the former Secretary of State Henry Kissinger once said, Russia can no longer confront America frontally, but can do a hell of a lot to sabotage its interests. In this case, from the Caucasian and Caspian regions, Russia is promoting its goals in South and Central Asia and is trying to undermine the supply of oil and gas to the West. And that takes us from geopolitics to eco-politics.

RUSSIA AND THE ENERGY ASSAULT ON EUROPE

In 2012 Vladimir Putin was reelected president of Russia. His leadership style is authoritarian, reflecting both his KGB background and Russia's need for strong leaders. Putin may even be tempted to remake the Soviet Union, but being unable to reconstruct it, his policies aim at extending Russia's economic influence over Europe. This is mostly done through new oil and gas supplies and two cases in point are the North Stream and the South Stream projects. *Google* and *Wikipedia* have a good number of articles illustrating the struggle between the European Union, which wants to diversify its sources of energy, and Moscow, which aims at "chaining" Europe with pipe and gas lines to make it dependent on Russia.

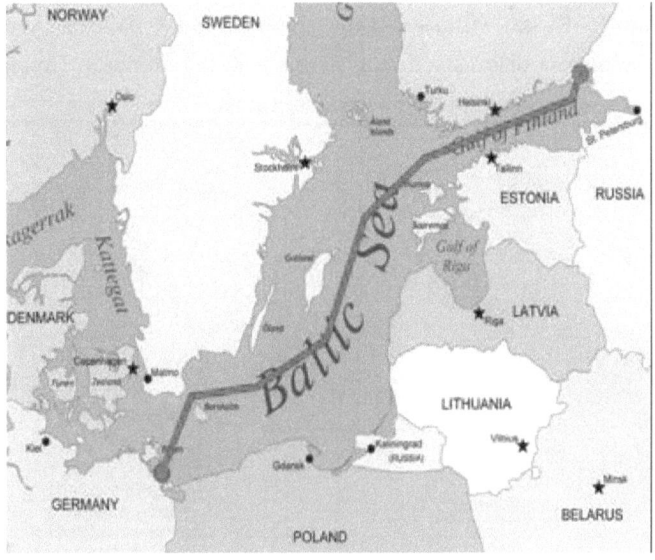

The North Stream Project. Source: Wikipedia

Europe is highly developed economically, but is poor from an energy point of view. Russia is poorly developed, but it has huge energy resources. The two should naturally complement each other, except that Moscow's goal is not only economic. And politically, the European Union and Russia do not see eye to eye. Hence, the cat and mouse play between them. Traditionally, Russia exports gas and oil to Europe through the Ukraine, but Ukraine is trying to get away from Moscow's tutelage. Politically, Moscow is controlling Ukraine for now, but in the long run it does not trust Kiev and is doing what it takes to bypass it. To this effect, Moscow has designed the North Stream gas line to reach Western Europe. In order to avoid a total dependence on Moscow energy sources, the European Union designed the Nabucco project. Russia, however, countered with the South Stream project. And this project is not only geo-economic; it is also political and geopolitical. Through the South Stream

181

project Russia will also regain a foothold in the Balkans. And the present dissatisfaction of Serbia with the European Union plays very well into the interests of Russia.

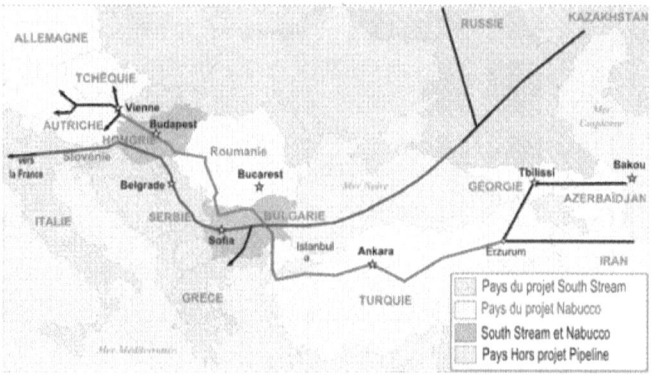

The South Stream and the Nabucco Projects. Source: Wikipedia

For centuries Moscow's dream was to control the Balkan Peninsula and to get a foothold on the Mediterranean Sea. Historically, Bulgaria was Russia's best friend in the region and Yugoslavia was Russia's best hope to reach the Mediterranean Sea. Romania, however, was in Russia's way and Moscow has tried several times to dismember it. Now, Romania is worried again. After joining NATO and after agreeing to accept the American anti-missile shield on its territory, Moscow has tried hard to isolate and weaken Romania. Indeed, both Russian projects, the North and the South Stream, leave Romania outside the European energy loop. Bucharest did join the Nabucco project, but it found itself again outmaneuvered by Moscow.

According to *Google* research, the North Stream gas line starts in Vyborg, Russia, bypasses the three Baltic Republics and Poland through the Baltic Sea, and reaches Germany directly. From there, the gas line, which is now operational, connects with Western Europe. On the other hand, while the Nabucco project is still in the planning stage, the South Stream project is about to start being built. In order to impose the project, Moscow negotiated with every country in the region. In 2008 Bulgaria was the first one to sign an agreement with Moscow and eventually all south-eastern European countries, except Romania, were lured to adhere to the project.

An article published in *Romania Libera* on November 2, 2012, explained that the project is financed 50 percent by Gazprom, a giant Russian company linked to the government, 20 percent by the Italian consortium Eni, 15 percent by the German firm Wintershall Holding, and 15 percent by the French company EDF. Lenin, the founder of the USSR, once said that the capitalists would sell the rope with which they will be hanged. Not far from true! Meanwhile, Gazprom announced that the work which was supposed to start in December 2013 would start in December 2012. The last two countries to join the project were Hungary and Serbia.

Traditionally, Serbia has been a pro-Russian country, but its main interests in the modern era were with Europe. Several recent events, however, have put Serbia on the spot. First, it was the dismemberment of Yugoslavia, which was difficult for Serbs to swallow. Then, it was the independence of Kosovo, which to this day is almost impossible to accept for most Serbs. And finally, Serbia encountered steep difficulties recently when trying to join the EU. All these have thrown Serbia into the open arms of Russia.

The new Serbian leaders, President Tomislav Nikolici and Prime Minister Ivica Dacici, are now pursuing an open pro-Russian policy. As *Romania Libera* of October 10, 2012, wrote, the Russians do not have to invade the Balkans anymore; they are now invited by Belgrade to come to the Balkans. Indeed, a Russo-Serbian partnership is already in the making. The Russians may be coming with oil and gas, but their real goal is geopolitical. For now, Serbia has already obtained a one billion dollars loan from Putin with more loans to follow soon. The Romanian newspaper stressed that for the time being the Russians are establishing economic bases, but in the future they may acquire military bases. And this time, there is no one to oppose Russia. Western Europe needs the energy; the European Union is wrestling with financial problems; and apparently the United States is still trying to redefine and hopefully to "re-reset" its relations with Moscow.

There are also other political, economic and geopolitical problems between Russia and the West. The new European politicians in Brussels, many of them of leftist orientation, tend to court Moscow on the one hand and to defer to Berlin on the other. Germany, by far the strongest EU power, is flexing again its muscles and is dealing now directly with Russia bypassing the interests of the Eastern European countries. And these are the same countries that in the past were victimized by both Russia and Germany. At the same time, the United States is increasingly trying to appease Moscow, ignoring the fears of the Eastern European nations. As a direct result, the once strongly pro-American bloc of East European countries is becoming cynical and may end up joining the anti-American chorus. Is this the foreign policy that Washington wants to project and promote in the area? At the beginning of WWII some eastern people felt liberated from under Soviet control. In time, however, they began to see the true colors of the Germans and some of them dared to tell them that they do not know how to make friends. The Germans answered arrogantly: we do not need friends, we have the Panzer. And as the saying goes, the rest is history . . .

IV — China and Southeast Asia

There is no country that has shaped more the process of globalization than China. *Made in China* is no longer just an indication; it is like a brand that permeates the entire planet. China is conquering the world!

The recent evolution of China, and also of East and Southeast Asia, reflects very much the traditional energy, the rich history, and the old values and work ethics of the region. Yet, the modern development of this vast area occurred under a high degree of governmental paternalistic and protectionist policies. As a rule the people of this region are hard working, disciplined, frugal, clannish and ethno-centric. Unlike people in the West, they obey and trust more the governments and also expect more from them. At the same time, far eastern people put more emphasis on family values and collective rights rather than individualism and personal rights as the West does. Yet, each country is different, cooperation among them is selective and even reluctant and regional blocs and integrations are rather loose. Nevertheless, China, Japan, South Korea, Taiwan and Singapore, as well as a few other Southeast Asian countries, have taken full advantage of the opportunities offered by globalization. And during the last several decades the rise of China has been impressive. A multitude of Chinese goods have penetrated the entire world from the big cities to the remotest corners of the planet. Almost anything we buy these days is made in China. Is this going to last?

THE RISE OF CHINA

It should be remembered that at one point in the past China was the most developed country in the world and its contribution to global progress was truly unique. Now, history appears to repeat itself. During the last two decades of the 20th Century China developed at a rate of 8 percent annually, and after that, it managed to still keep a high rate of development even when the rest of the world went into recession. As a result, it took Britain more than 100 years and the United States some 30 years to double their per capita output and income, but it took China only 10 years to do it.

Today's China has very much returned to its traditional roots and cultural values emphasizing order, authority, and work. Rearmed with the old attitudes, China took advantage of the diligence of its people, learned new Western technology, and began to inch ahead. However, China still has many shortcomings and has a long way to go. Widespread poverty is one of them. By comparison to the United States, the Chinese per capita GNP is about six-seven times smaller. Will China ever catch up? And if it does, what will the economic consequences be at a global scale? Another downfall is China's largely unfavorable natural environment. China has only 0.1 hectares of cropland per person, which is half the world average, and its fertile lands are crowded with too many people. From a demographic point of view, China is also close to reaching the maximum carrying capacity of its lands while the population is still increasing.

Economically, China's achievements are traced back to the late 1970s policy of Deng Xiaoping, which emphasized developing agriculture, industry, science, and defense. And that policy of development and modernization succeeded to the point that it began to make its neighbors nervous. In this vein, if geopolitically the region was threatened by Japan in the past, now China's evolution is seen with uneasiness. To calm down its neighbors, according to Jacobson's book *Old Nations, New World*, the same Deng Xiaoping advanced the slogan that "*the stronger China grows the better the chances are for preserving world peace.*" And he envisioned a multipolar world with five pillars: China, the United States, Russia, Germany and Japan. During a short period of time, Deng liberalized China economically, transformed it domestically, and imposed it internationally. Deng's policies also changed people's attitude, reshaped the country, and placed China again not only in the middle of the world as during the classical *Middle Kingdom*, but close to the top of the world as well.

Since liberalization, China has enjoyed steady economic growths, has surpassed recently the economy of Japan, and it may even surpass the economic output of the United States in about 2 or 3 decades. In the process, the Beijing government acted with an iron fist initially, but the grip has been slowly loosening. Like Japan in the past and South Korea more recently, the authorities encouraged the export industries. As a consequence, during the period of unprecedented growth from 1970 to 1990 the GNP share of its exports increased from 5 percent to almost 36 percent. All this time Beijing encouraged foreign investments, but it retained a higher degree of control over the companies that invested in China. In the process, according to the December 2005 issue of *Spectator*, China began to move from low-tech into medium-tech and even into some high technology fields. As a result of this steady development, over the last 3 or 4 decades the proportion of the poor Chinese people, living on about one dollar a day, was reduced from 64 percent to 17 percent. This is considered without precedent.

East Asia

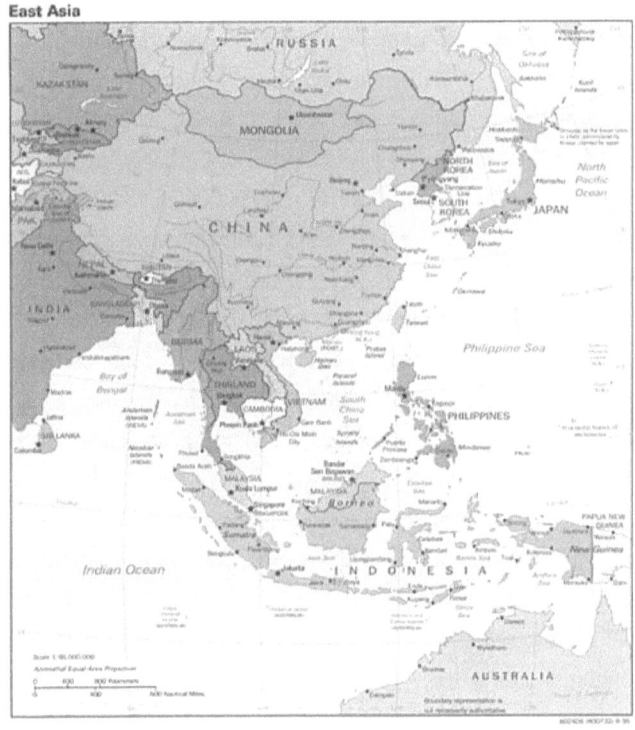

Source: Wikipedia, the free Encyclopedia

The *Economist* of December 15, 2012, describes, for example, how the evolution of one giant company has contributed to the recent change of the country. The Chinese industrial complex Can Foxconn is currently the largest manufacturer in the world. The company's main facility is located in Shenzhen in southern China and employs 240,000 people. In addition, the company has 28 other plants throughout China and employs a total of 1.4 million workers. They manufacture electronic parts and sub-assemblies for a number of Western firms with the American company Apple being the most important of them. Currently, the industrial giant is looking toward further expansion and toward moving from low-tech products to higher tech products. China does have the brain capacity and the labor force to move forward. From a "brain" point of view, for example, the same magazine reveals that as of 2011 China had the largest number of patent applications in the world. According to the *UN World Intellectual Property Organization*, in 2011 China received 526,412 applications, exceeding the United States, Japan and South Korea, the next three countries to apply for new patents. However, Can Foxconn has a hard time finding skilled workers necessary for high-end products. That shows that China is entering a period of industrial maturity which in the future will come most likely with problems similar to those encountered by the Western countries: demand for better working conditions and higher salaries, which in turn will raise production cost and will make Chinese goods less competitive globally.

Although developing fast, the Chinese economy is still far behind when compared to the Western countries. Nevertheless, China is now ahead of many of its neighbors, such as Indonesia, the Philippines, or Burma. It should be stressed that a very large number of Chinese resettled in Southeast Asia in recent history where many of them became businessmen, but where they have also experienced periodic rejection. Those rejections made the ethnic Chinese very clannish and forced them to live mostly in segregated neighborhoods. However, the Chinese are good entrepreneurs and risk takers and have taken over a good part of the local business. Furthermore, their businesses are done through personal inter-Chinese connections known as the "bamboo network." Beijing calls this connection between China and the Southeast Asian Chinese communities a "co-prosperity zone." Occasionally, local people reject the Chinese entrepreneurship and success, but more often they benefit from their Chinese minorities and their special links with China.

Politically and economically, modern China remains a centrally controlled system with a mixed private and socialist economy. The *Economist* of 5 January 2012 stresses in this regard that currently the Beijing leaders are trying to present "a friendlier public face, but oppose bold new demands for democratic reforms." Yet, economically, the government has reduced its ownership to less than half of China's activities. Most of the business is now in private hands, but this situation creates some problems. It entails an antagonism between modernizers, who look at the world globally, and isolationists, who would rather turn their focus inside. China is also confronted with a potential conflict between the old political leaders and the new private business owners. This latter conflict is already brewing. In addition, the current economic development is very uneven within the country, which constitutes a source of friction. There is a strong contrast between the eastern areas of China which were opened for international business and the hinterland of the country where most people live in poverty in rural areas.

The fast development of the eastern seaboard has also resulted in a high degree of social and economic polarization with a profound contrast between the newly rich and the working masses that have arrived from the interior. Worse still, working conditions in the developed areas are often unbearable. People work long hours for the equivalent of 25 US cents per hour and often live in prison-like conditions. As a matter of fact, China also has about one thousand prisons with millions of inmates who are forced to work. Several journalists have pointed out that in some parts of the country even young children are exploited. In his book *The Late Great USA,* Jerome Corsi offers the example of the New Balance Tennis shoes, which are made in China's Factory Nr. 5. The shoes are manufactured for under 10 dollars a pair, come to the US at 14.61 dollars, and sell for an average of 135 dollars a pair. New Balance makes huge profits from exploiting prisoners and children. Because it is known under what conditions these shoes are manufactured, Corsi considers that America has lost its moral authority to protest or to invoke human rights. The situation is similar in most Southeast Asian countries.

Japan. In spite of China's recent progress, Japan remains an economic giant with global reaches in many fields. It is worth remembering in this case that post-war Japan was ruined. Yet, it was rebuilt with American assistance and by virtue of its people's patriotism. In this regard, the United States helped Japan and sacrificed itself for the sake of expanding political influence and for opposing Soviet global ambitions. Japan was also helped by its own traditions. Many Japanese businesses treated the workers like families: employees would work for a lifetime for a company and the company would take good care of them.

The Japanese economy was also reorganized and rebuilt through cooperation between private business, unions, and governmental institutions. The government was strongly protectionist and it directed and shaped the national economy through the powerful Ministry of Trade and Industry (MITI) which later became the Ministry of Economy, Trade and Industry (METI). It was a planned economic development oriented toward exports, and the government helped with subsidies and through the devaluation of the national currency. In post-war Japan hard work and quality were like religion. With passage of time, Japan excelled in many industrial fields and even managed to out-compete the West. The results were impressive. Correspondingly, the Japanese standard of living reached western levels. With full industrial maturity, however, Japan began to experience some of the problems of the West and even recessions. But, Japan has managed the impossible: to have a piece of cake and to eat too. Japan is now in many ways a Western-type of country, but it has also kept its old traditions. The result is that technologically, Japan is now one of the most advanced countries in the world.

South Korea has copied Japan, has benefited from American help and protection, and has become a strong new comer in today's global economy. Similar to Japan, which was destroyed at the end of World War II, South Korea was thoroughly ravaged during the 1950-1953 war triggered by North Korea. Yet, it made one of the most spectacular economic recoveries in the world. The key to South Korean recovery was nationalism and authoritarian regimes. Indeed, between 1948 and 1988 the country was ruled directly by the military or indirectly by military-backed governments.

In order to recover, the government initiated land reforms and applied a policy of controlled development through five-year plans. Those who remember the five-year communist plans may turn their noses. It all depends on the quality of the leaders at the top and on the hard work of the people at the bottom. For decades the Korean people worked up to 60 hours a week and strikes were practically banned. The government granted subsidies to key industries, protected them against foreign competition, and like Japan, encouraged exports. While criticizing the former military governments, *Time* magazine of December 17, 2012 gave them credit for their economic achievements. Tiny South Korea has now the 11th economy in the world. Under those conditions, South Korea started with low quality products, but slowly moved into medium and high quality ones. Samsung, for example, has already supplanted Japan as the electronic leading force in East Asia.

While the government helped with specific policies, business leaders were scouting the globe for new niches to fill and occupy. For example, the Korean auto industry is now respected globally, but it took several decades to arrive. Currently, while the KIA cars are directed toward lower and middle income buyers, Hyundai competes with the expensive Japanese cars, and the manufacturers are already eying the luxury niches. More recently, South Korean began to liberalize somehow its economy, but to this day Seoul is wary of foreign investments. Sovereignty and nationalism are highly priced and the people are proud of their achievements. Correspondingly, the South Korean standards of living are similar now to any Western standards. By comparison, North Korea looks like hell, and it is hell on earth.

Does the world have something to learn from the recent East Asian extraordinary achievements? We should remember that Japan is virtually devoid of mineral resources and yet, it has one of the most developed economies in the world. China, on the other hand, has an unforgiving nature in many areas and is overpopulated, but it is now a huge economic success. As for South Korea, this small country has become a big economic miracle with a global impact. These three countries have achieved wonders through hard work and discipline under competent and responsible leaders. This is what the West can and should learn from the East! Work, discipline and honest leadership!

Does the world have anything to fear from them and especially from China? History teaches us that as a rule the *Middle Kingdom* has always been a peaceful giant that wanted to be respected rather than feared. And China must be respected! The real danger to the world does not come from China. It is posed by the Middle East.

The Middle East is very important to the world in several ways. From a globalization point of view, it is a crucial source of oil and gas, and this energy is indispensable to the very existence of our modern civilization. Economically, the Middle East is also important as a vital link between Europe, Asia, and Africa. From a political and geopolitical point of view, however, the Middle East is highly unstable and is a cauldron of ethnic and religious conflicts that pose great perils to global peace.

Currently, the biggest problems in the Middle East are caused by the plight of the Palestinian people, thus the conflict between Israel and the Arabs, and by the nuclear ambitions of Iran, which may trigger an Israeli preemptive attack and possibly a global disaster. Is a catastrophe imminent? Is there a solution? What will the super powers do if a peaceful solution will not be found? The current process of economic globalization is not directly affected by the Middle East, but a catastrophe there would put an end to those who dream of full globalization.

Selected Bibliography and Footnotes

PART ONE—GENERAL TOPICS

A good part of the sources of this study are indicated within the text. Some sources are not specified if they represent common knowledge, but others are footnoted individually. Many of them come from the following very good and highly recommended books:

Manfred B. Steger, *Globalization*, NY, London: Sterling, 2007

Peter Dicken, *Global Shift* (*Mapping the Changing Contour of World Economy*) NY, London: The Guilford Press, 2007

David Rothkopf, *Superclass* (*The Global Power Elite and the World they are making*) NY: Farrar, Straus and Giroux, 2008

Daron Acemoglu, James A. Robinson, *The Origins of Power, Prosperity, and Poverty: Why Nations Fail,* New York: Crown Business, 2012

Patrick J. Buchanan, *The Great Betrayal,* NY, Boston, Toronto, London: Little, Brown and Co., 1998

Jerome E. Corsi, *The Late Great USA*, Los Angeles: WND Books, 2007

Nicholas Dima, *Culture, Religion and Geopolitics*, Bloomington: Exlibris, 2010

Nicholas Dima, *Cross Cultural Communication,* Washington, DC: Institute for the Study of Man, 1990

Footnotes

(1) Steger, p. 10 and 19

(2) Some of the adages were taken from Rothkopf

(3) Steger, op. cit. pp. 14-19 and Dicken, in passim

(4) Dicken, pp. 318-338

(5) Steger, p. 163

(6) Ibid, p. 124

(7) Acemoglu and Robinson, p. 131

(8) Buchanan, p. 58

(9) Dicken, p. 89

(10) Ibid, pp. 38-43

(11) Acemoglu and Robinson, p. 79

(12) See articles on Bretton Woods, *Wikipedia*; also Steger, pp. 50-55

(13) Dicken, pp. 537-538

(14) Cited by Steger, p. 53

(15) Dicken, p. 190

(16) Ibid, pp. 232-242

(17) Cited by Rothkopf, p. 107

(18) Dicken, p 538; as well as current media

(19) Rothkopf, p. 278; the author has a good overview of secret societies

(20) Dima, *Culture, Religion and Geopolitics*, pp. 92-93

(21) Rothkopf, p. 195

(22)Dima, *Culture, Religion and Geopolitics*, pp. 37-38

(23) Rothkopf, p. 12

(24) Dicken, p. 443

(25) Rothkopf, p. 19

(26) Ibid, pp. 32-37

(27) Ibid, p. 49

(28) cited by Rothkopf, p. 240

(29) Nicholas Dima, *Cross Cultural Communication,* Chapters 1 and 7

(30) Steger, p. 100

(31) Buchanan, p. 55

(32) Dicken, p. 366

(33) Ibid, pp. 255-259

(34) Ibid, especially pp. 278-315

(35) Ibid, especially pp. 402-406

(36) Steger, p. 129

(37) Ibid, p.154

(38) Ibid, p. 145

(39) Buchanan, p. 288

(40) Ibid, pp. 72-74

(41) Ibid, p. 51

(42) Cited by Buchanan, p. 286

(43) Acemoglu and Robinson, in passim

(44) Nicholas Dima, *Cross Cultural Communication*, Chap. 1

(45) Mark R. Levin, *Liberty and Tyranny*, NY: Simon and Shuster, 2009, p. 24

(46) Acemoglu and Robinson, Op. Cit. p. 436

(47) Cited by Buchanan, p. 108

(48) Rothkopf, pp. 321-323

OTHER RECOMMENDED BIBLIOGRAPHY:

David S. Landes, *The Wealth and Poverty of Nations,* NY, London: Norton and co. 1998

Samuel P. Huntington, *The Clash of Civilizations and the Remaking of World Order,* New York: Simon & Shuster, 1996

Dani Rodrik, *The Global Paradox, Democracy and the Future of the World Economy*, New York: W.W. Norton & Company, 2011

Wikipedia, Almanacs, Encyclopedias, the Internet, and other modern sources.

Selected and Recommended Bibliography

PART TWO—REGIONAL STUDIES

EUROPE AND THE EUROPEAN UNION

The World Almanac and Book of Facts, World Almanac Books, New York: 2007

Wikipedia—The Free Encyclopedia, 2008-2012

Lindsay Jenkins, *Britain Held Hostage*, Washington, DC: Orange State Press, 1997

Personal discussions with many people and leaders, including doctor Vasile Puscas, chief negotiator of Romania for EU integration

Samuel Huntington, *The Clash of Civilizations and the Remaking of World Order*, New York: Simon & Shuster, 1996

Various internet entries on EU such as: http://www. european-unon.com; http://www.europeanconstitution.le/ termsused.asp; and http://www.delidn.ec.europa.eu/en/ eu_guide/eu_guide_2.htm; and others

USA AND NAFTA

Robert Pastor, *Toward a North American Community—Lessons from the Old World for the New*, Washington, DC: Institute for International Economics, 2001

Vicente Fox and Rob Allyn, *Revolution of Hope*, New York: Viking, 2007

Robert Pastor, "*A North American Community Approach to Security*," Testimony before the Subcommittee on the Western Hemisphere, U. S. Senate Foreign Relations Committee, June 9, 2005

Jerome A. Corsi, *The Late Great USA*, Los Angeles: WND Books, 2007

Peter Hakim, Robert E. Litan, Ed. *The Future of North American Integration, Beyond NAFTA,* Washington, DC: Brookings Institution Press, 2002

Chuck Hagel, *America—Our Next Chapter*, New York: Harper Collins Publishers, 2008

Samuel P. Huntington, *The Clash of Civilizations and the Remaking of World Order*, New York: Simon and Schuster, 1996

Sidney Weintraub Ed., *NAFTA's Impact on North America—The First Decade*, Washington, DC: Center for Strategies and International Studies, 2006

RUSSIA: OLD GEOPOLITICS AND NEW ECONOMIC REALITIES

Nicholas Dima, *Moldova and the Transdnestr Republic*, NY: East European Monographs, Columbia University Press, 2001

Nicholas Dima, "The Moldovan-Dnestr Republic: A Geopolitical Game," *The Journal for Social, Political and Economic Studies*, Spring 1999

Nicholas Dima, various articles on http://www.sfppr

Samuel Huntington, *The Clash of Civilizations and the Remaking of World Order*, New York: Simon & Shuster, 1996

Leon Aron, *Yeltsin: a Revolutionary Life,* NY: St. Martin Press, 2000

Marek Jan Chodakiewicz, *Intermarium, the Lands between the Black and Baltic Seas*, New Brunswick, US, and London, UK: Transaction Publishers, 2012

CHINA AND SOUTHEAST ASIA

Nicholas Dima, *Culture, Religion, and Geopolitics*, Bloomington: Exlibris, 2010

Samuel P. Huntington, *The Clash of Civilizations and the Remaking of World Order,* New York: Simon & Shuster, 1996

David Jacobson, *Old Nations, New World,* NY: Westview Press, 1994

Jerome E. Corsi, *The Late Great USA*, Los Angeles: WND Books, 2007

David S. Landes, *The Wealth and Poverty of Nations,* NY, London: Norton and Co. 1998

www.ingramcontent.com/pod-product-compliance
Lightning Source LLC
Chambersburg PA
CBHW030319290526
45785CB00001B/430

* 9 7 8 1 4 7 9 7 8 0 9 4 5 *